Hiking

Colorado's Indian Peaks Wilderness

Help Us Keep This Guide Up to Date

Every effort has been made by the author and editors to make this guide as accurate and useful as possible. However, many things can change after a guide is published—trails are rerouted, regulations change, techniques evolve, facilities come under new management, and so on.

We would love to hear from you concerning your experiences with this guide and how you feel it could be improved and kept up to date. While we may not be able to respond to all comments and suggestions, we'll take them to heart and we'll also make certain to share them with the authors. Please send your comments and suggestions to the following address:

The Globe Pequot Press
Reader Response/Editorial Department
P.O. Box 480
Guilford, CT 06437

Or you may e-mail us at:

editorial@globe-pequot.com

Thanks for your input, and happy travels!

Hiking

Colorado's Indian Peaks Wilderness

Bob D'Antonio

FALCON®

GUILFORD, CONNECTICUT

An imprint of The Globe Pequot Press

This book is dedicated to my best friend and wife, Laurel,
and to Nala, my wonderful Labrador Retriever.
Thanks for all those special times in the mountains.

*A*FALCON GUIDE®

Maps by Trapper Badovinac
Photos by Bob D'Antonio
Illustrations on pp. 12–13 from *Bear Aware* (FalconGuide) by Bill Schneider.

Library of Congress Cataloging-in-Publication Data is Available.

ISBN 0-7627-1107-8

Manufactured in the United States of America
First Edition/First Printing

Contents

Acknowledgments

A book of this scope would not have been possible without the help and support of many fine people.

Thanks to Glen Cook of the Boulder Ranger District, Gary Neptune, owner of Neptune Mountaineering, and Mark Haber for being understanding of my schedule at work.

To all the folks who volunteer time working on trails, a heartfelt thanks. And to all the rangers and folks at the Boulder and Sulphur Ranger Districts, thanks for all your time and effort in keeping the Indian Peaks a wild and beautiful place.

Colorful aspens near the Hessie trailhead.

Map Legend

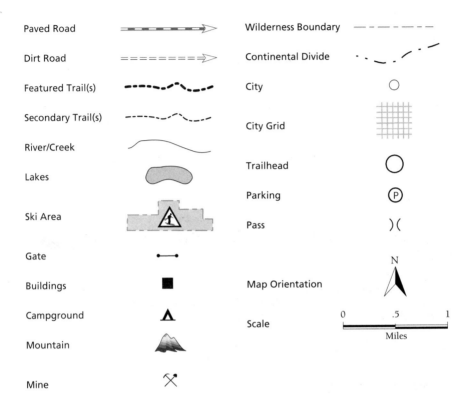

Paved Road	
Dirt Road	
Featured Trail(s)	
Secondary Trail(s)	
River/Creek	
Lakes	
Ski Area	
Gate	
Buildings	
Campground	
Mountain	
Mine	

Wilderness Boundary	
Continental Divide	
City	
City Grid	
Trailhead	
Parking	
Pass	
Map Orientation	
Scale	

Overview Map

Backcountry Zones and Hikes

To Estes Park

ROCKY MOUNTAIN NATIONAL PARK

1
2
Allensprak

SR 72

ROARING FORK BZ

34

Lake Granby

HELL CANYON BZ

MIDDLE ST. VRAIN BZ
6

CR 102

BUCHANAN BZ

7 5 4   3
8
Camp   Peaceful
Dick   Valley

35
36

INDIAN

CONEY CREEK
BZ   9

12

CASCADE CREEK BZ

11

PEAKS

CRATER
LAKE BZ

Brainard Lake Road

10

WILDERNESS

13 16
14 17
15 18

Ward

AREA

CR 129

FOUR LAKES BZ

37
38

ARAPAHO BZ

19

SR 72

COLUMBINE BZ

20
21

40

NEVA BZ

GLACIER BZ

23 24

CR 128

CASPER LAKE BZ

CR 111

Fraser

DEVILS THUMB BZ
WOODLAND BZ

Nederland

Hessie
25   22 Eldora
26
27 28 29
31   30

119

To
Boulder

Winter
Park

MIDDLE BOULDER BZ

CR 149

Rollinsville

32
33 East
Portal

Introduction

The Indian Peaks Wilderness is a spectacular area of high peaks, stunning alpine lakes, and flower-filled meadows that extends from the southern boundary of Rocky Mountain National Park in the north to Rollins Pass in the south. The Indian Peaks Wilderness Area encompasses 73,391 acres of alpine grandeur and extends almost 19 miles in a north/south direction and 16 miles in an east/west direction. The area was designated a wilderness in 1978 and since that time has become one of America's most popular wilderness areas, which sees heavy use in the summer months. The Indian Peaks lies a mere 55 miles north of Denver and 25 miles west of Boulder. Elevation of the Indian Peaks ranges from a low point of 8,400 feet to a high of more than 13,500 feet above sea level. There are six major trails, passes, and routes that connect the eastern and western areas of the wilderness. Caribou (11,851 feet) and Arapaho (11,906 feet) Passes lie near the southern boundary of the wilderness area near Mount Neva and North and South Arapaho Peaks. Almost dead center is Pawnee Pass (12,541 feet), the highest pass in the Indian Peaks Wilderness Area. Buchanan Pass (11,837 feet) is in the northern portion of the wilderness area and connects its northeast and northwest sections.

There are three major ecological zones in the Indian Peaks Wilderness Area: the montane zone, the subalpine zone, and the alpine zone. The montane zone occupies less than 10 percent of the Indian Peaks Wilderness Area, mostly on the western side near Monarch Lake. Aspen, lodgepole pine, and Douglas fir are the most common trees in this zone. Wildlife that call this area home include: black bear, mule deer, coyote, squirrel, mountain lion,

Northerly view from Caribou Pass.

beaver, and rabbit. Common flowers in the montane zone are the Colorado columbine, Indian paintbrush, and tall chiming bell.

The subalpine zone exits at elevations between 9,000 and 11,000 feet. More than half of the Indian Peaks Wilderness Area lies in this zone. Common trees in this zone are aspen, lodgepole pine, and subalpine fir. Wildlife similar to the montane zone call this area home and delight in the dense forests, open meadows, and cool streams. The subalpine zone offers hikers shelter of tall mature trees, rolling streams, and abundant, colorful wildflowers.

The alpine zone encompasses more than 30 percent of the Indian Peaks Wilderness Area. This is an area of snowfields, scree slopes, glacier-fed lakes, and hardy plant life. The landscape above 11,000 feet seems at first glance to be extremely barren; nothing could be further from the truth. This is an area of complex plant and animal life that have adapted and thrive in a harsh yet beautiful environment. Tread lightly in this zone; stay on the trail and off the tundra vegetation.

The Indian Peaks Wilderness is one of America's most popular wilderness areas for good reasons. The trails are well maintained, the views are spectacular, the alpine lakes and streams offer great fishing in a remote environment, and the high peaks are nothing short of stunning. Don't let the summer crowds keep you from visiting and enjoying the wilderness area. Midweek is a great time to explore as the heavy weekend crowds have all but disappeared. Late spring and early fall are also a great times to visit, as are the winter months. Strap on a pair of snowshoes or skis and enjoy the backcountry in the solitude that only winter offers.

Any of the trails in this book are a worthwhile excursion into the backcountry. From short, one-day hikes to multiday backpacking trips, treks into the Indian Peaks will enchant you and draw you back time and time again. The hikes and the trails in this book are some of my favorite and hopefully will become yours. This book will help enhance your experience in the Indian Peaks Wilderness Area.

I have spent a tremendous amount of time in and around the Indian Peaks Wilderness Area and enjoyed almost every moment. I have met a number of fine folks on the trails who share the same respect and love for this very special area. The Indian Peaks center me. They put me in my place and show me that I am part of an incredible and diverse world. Living near Boulder, I see the Indian Peaks almost every day. I like that. They put a smile on my face and raise my spirits. I see them in different lights and in different seasons. They are stunning. They are constant. They are beautiful. Enjoy!

TRAIL ETIQUETTE

The Indian Peaks Wilderness is an extremely popular place for hikers, anglers, and horseback riders. The trails can become quite crowded, especially on summer weekends, so it is more than likely you will encounter other trail users on your hike. If you encounter a horseback rider, please take note: Horseback riders always have the right-of-way. Move down and to the right of the trail. Don't make any sudden moves or noises as horses spook easily in tight situations, and give the horse enough room to maneuver.

As we all know, hiking uphill can be a lot harder than hiking downhill. Downhill hikers should always give the right-of-way to the uphill hiker. If you are the uphill hiker and want to take a breather, move off to the right and let the downhill hiker pass. Don't be afraid to say hello to other trail users when you are out on the trail.

If you are hiking with a dog, please control your pet at all times. In the Indian Peaks this means that your dog must be on a leash at all times.

There is a reason why I travel into the wilderness: I cherish the quiet time in the backcountry. I love the sounds of wild streams, songbirds, bugling elk, and the wind blowing through the aspen trees. Hike as quietly as possible. Keep a low profile and avoid disturbing other trail users.

Trails

There are twenty-eight maintained trails in the Indian Peak Wilderness covering more than 133 miles. The trails range in distance from 0.6 mile (Rainbow Lakes Trail) to 15.6 miles (Buchanan Pass Trail). A majority of the trails in the wilderness are marked and easy to follow, and most are of moderate difficulty and see heavy use during the summer months. The trails in the wilderness are rocky and range in elevation from 8,280 feet to more than 13,100 feet. Please stay on all marked trails; cutting or making new trails causes unsightly marks on the landscape, leaving ugly scars and serving no useful purpose. Good campsites can be found along a majority of the trails, where permitted.

Peaks

The Indian Peaks Wilderness Areas has thirty-five peaks. Ellsworth Bethel (1863–1925), a Denver school teacher, named the Indian Peaks after various Native American tribes that played an important part in Colorado's early history. Of the thirty-five peaks, thirty-two are more than 11,000 feet, twenty-three are more than 12,000 feet, and seven tower high above the Colorado Front Range to more than 13,000 feet. North Arapaho Peak, at 13,502 feet above sea level, is the highest peak in the wilderness.

Water

There are more than fifty named and unnamed lakes in the wilderness, covering more than 500 acres. Most of the lakes can be reached by trail, and all the lakes can be fished for various trout. There are also fifteen named streams in the wilderness and numerous unnamed streams and tributaries, most of which contain trout.

BACKCOUNTRY REGULATIONS

- Get a wilderness permit for all overnight use (see Appendix A).

- Camp only in appropriate places (see Zero Impact).

- Stay on trails (where possible) and don't create shortcuts.

- Dispose of human waste in a cat hole at least 200 feet from all water sources and campsites. Dispose of bathwater and dishwater well away from water sources.

- Use campstoves rather than cooking fires whenever possible.

- Carry out all trash. If you can pack it in, you can pack it out.

- Limit group size to ten people or less.

- Suspend food out of reach of animals. Do not leave behind food scraps.

- Do not feed or in any way disturb the wildlife.

- Do not operate any mechanized vehicle in the wilderness.

- Do not destroy, deface, disturb, or remove from its natural setting any plant, rock, animal, or archaeological resource.

Please read the Zero Impact section below for more details on minimizing impact on the wilderness.

ZERO IMPACT

Going into a wild area is like visiting a museum. You obviously do not want to leave your mark on an art treasure in the museum. If everybody going through the museum left one little mark, the piece of art would be quickly destroyed—and of what value is a big building full of trashed art? The same goes for pristine wildlands. If we all left just one little mark on the landscape, the backcountry would soon be spoiled. A wilderness can accommodate human use as long as everybody behaves, but a few thoughtless or uninformed visitors can ruin it for everybody who follows. All backcountry users have a responsibility to follow the rules of zero-impact camping. Nowadays most wilderness users want to walk softly, but some aren't aware that they have poor manners. Often their actions are dictated by the outdated habits of a past generation of campers who cut green boughs for evening shelters, built campfires with fire rings, and dug trenches around tents. In the 1950s, these practices may have been acceptable, but they are not today as they leave long-lasting scars.

Because wild places are becoming rare and the number of users is mushrooming, a new code of ethics is growing out of the necessity of coping with the unending waves of people who want a perfect backcountry experience. Today, we all must leave no mark that we were there by following the principles of zero impact:

- Leave with everything you brought in.

- Leave no sign of your visit.

- Leave the landscape as you found it.

Most of us know better than to litter—in or out of the backcountry. Be sure you leave nothing, regardless of how small it is, along the trail or at your campsite. This means you should pack out everything, including orange peels, flip tops, cigarette butts, and gum wrappers. Also, pick up any trash that others leave behind.

Follow the main trail. Avoid cutting switchbacks and walking on vegetation beside the trail. Don't pick up "souvenirs," such as rocks, antlers, or wildflowers. The next person wants to see them, too, and collecting such items violates many regulations.

Avoid making loud noises on the trail (unless you are in bear country) or in camp. Be courteous—remember, sound travels easily in the backcountry, especially across water.

Carry a lightweight trowel to bury human waste 6 to 8 inches deep at least 200 feet from any water source. Pack out used toilet paper.

Go without a campfire. Carry a stove for cooking and a flashlight, candle lantern, or headlamp for light. For emergencies, learn how to build a no-trace fire.

Camp in obviously used sites when they are available. Otherwise, camp and cook on durable surfaces such as bedrock, sand, gravel bars, or bare ground.

Leave nothing behind—and put your ear to the ground and listen carefully. Thousands of people coming behind you are thanking you for your courtesy and good sense.

MAKE IT A SAFE TRIP

The Boy Scouts of America has been guided for decades by what is perhaps the single best piece of safety advice: Be prepared. For starters, this means carrying survival and first-aid materials, proper clothing, compass, and topographic map—and knowing how to use them.

Perhaps the second-best piece of safety advice is to tell somebody where you're going and when you plan to return. Pilots must file flight plans before every trip, and anybody venturing into a blank spot on the map should do the same. File your "flight plan" with a friend or relative before taking off.

Close behind your flight plan and being prepared with proper equipment is physical conditioning. Being fit not only makes wilderness travel more fun, it makes it safer. Here are a few more tips:

- Check the weather forecast. Be careful not to get caught at high altitude by a bad storm or along a stream in a flash flood. Watch cloud formations closely so you don't get stranded on a ridgeline during a lightning storm. Avoid traveling during prolonged periods of cold weather.

- Avoid traveling alone in the wilderness and keep your party together.

- Don't exhaust yourself or other members of your party by traveling too far or too fast. Let the slowest person set the pace.

- Study basic survival and first aid before leaving home.

- Before you leave for the trailhead, find out as much as you can about the route, especially the potential hazards.

- Don't wait until you're confused to look at your maps. Follow them as you go along so you have a continual fix on your location.

- If you get lost, don't panic. Sit down and relax for a few minutes while you carefully check your topo map and take a compass reading. Confidently plan your next move. It's often smart to retrace your steps until you find familiar ground, even if you think it might lengthen your trip. Lots of people get temporarily lost in the wilderness and survive—usually by calmly and rationally dealing with the situation.

- Stay clear of all wild animals.

- Take a first-aid kit that includes, at a minimum, a sewing needle, snakebite kit, aspirin, antibacterial ointment, antiseptic swabs, butterfly bandages, adhesive tape, adhesive strips, gauze pads, two triangular bandages, codeine tablets, two inflatable splints, moleskin or Second Skin for blisters, 3-inch gauze, CPR shield, rubber gloves, and lightweight first-aid instructions.

- Take a survival kit that includes, at a minimum, a compass, whistle, matches in a waterproof container, cigarette lighter, candle, signal mirror, flashlight, fire starter, aluminum foil, water purification tablets, space blanket, and flare.

Lightning

Mountains are prone to sudden thunderstorms. If you get caught in a lightning storm, take special precautions. Remember:

- Take cover before a storm hits; lightning can travel ahead of a storm.

- Don't try to make it back to your vehicle. It isn't worth the risk. Instead, seek shelter even if it's only a short way back to the trailhead. Lightning storms usually don't last long, and from a safe vantage point, you might enjoy the sights and sounds.

- Be especially careful not to get caught on a mountaintop or exposed ridge; under large, solitary trees; in the open; or near standing water.

- Seek shelter in a low-lying area, ideally in a stand of small, uniformly sized trees.

- Avoid anything that attracts lightning, like metal tent poles, graphite fishing rods, or pack frames.

- Crouch with both feet firmly on the ground.

- Put your feet on your pack (as long as it doesn't have a metal frame) or sleeping pad for extra insulation against shock.

- Don't walk or huddle together with others in your group. Instead, stay 50 feet apart, so if somebody gets hit by lightning, others can give first aid.

- If you're in a tent, stay in your sleeping bag with your feet on your pad.

  For more information on lightning, log onto www.lightningsafety.com.

Hypothermia

Be aware of hypothermia, a condition in which the body's internal temperature drops below normal. It can lead to mental and physical collapse and death. Hypothermia is caused by exposure to cold and is aggravated by wetness, wind, and exhaustion. The moment you begin to lose heat faster than your body produces it, you're suffering from exposure. Your body starts involuntary exercise, such as shivering, to stay warm and makes adjustments to preserve normal temperature in vital organs, restricting bloodflow in the extremities. Both responses drain your energy reserves. The only way to stop the drain is to reduce the degree of exposure.

With full-blown hypothermia, as energy reserves are exhausted, cold blood reaches the brain, depriving you of good judgment and reasoning power. You won't be aware that this is happening. Without treatment your internal temperature slides downward, which will eventually lead to stupor, collapse, and death.

To defend against hypothermia, stay dry. When clothes get wet, they lose about 90 percent of their insulating value. Wool loses relatively less heat; cotton, down, and some synthetics lose more. Choose rain clothes that cover the head, neck, body, and legs and provide good protection against wind-driven rain. Most hypothermia cases develop in air temperatures between 30 and 50 degrees, but hypothermia can develop in warmer temperatures.

If your party is exposed to wind, cold, and wet, watch yourself and others for uncontrollable fits of shivering; vague, slow, or slurred speech; memory lapses; incoherence; immobile, fumbling hands; frequent stumbling or a lurching gait; drowsiness; apparent exhaustion; and inability to get up after a rest. When a member of your party has hypothermia, he may deny any problem. Believe the symptoms, not the victim. Even mild symptoms demand the following treatment:

- Get the victim out of the wind and rain.

- Strip off all wet clothes.

- If the victim is only mildly impaired, give her warm drinks. Then get the victim in warm clothes and a warm sleeping bag. Place well-wrapped water bottles filled with heated water close to the victim.

- If the victim is badly impaired, attempt to keep her awake. Put the victim in a sleeping bag with another person—both naked. If you have a double bag, put two warm people in with the victim.

Fording Rivers

Early summer hiking in the Indian Peaks Wilderness Area does involve crossing streams swollen with run-off. When done correctly and carefully, crossing a big river can be safe, but you must know your limits.

Know those cases where you simply should turn back. Even if only one member of your party (such as a child) might not be able to follow larger, stronger members, you might not want to try a risky ford. Never be embarrassed by being too cautious.

Jasper Lake.

One key to safely fording rivers is confidence. If you aren't a strong swimmer, you should be. This not only allows you to safely get across a river that is a little deeper and stronger than you thought, but it gives you the confidence to avoid panic, which can easily make a situation worse. Practice builds confidence. Find a warm-water river near your home and carefully practice crossing it both with a pack and without. You can also start with a smaller stream and work up to a major river. After you've become a strong swimmer, get used to swimming in the current.

When you get to the ford, carefully assess the situation. Don't automatically cross at the point where the trail comes to the stream and head on a straight line for the marker on the other side. A mountain river can change every spring during high run-off, so a ford that was safe last year might be too deep this year. Study upstream and downstream and look for a place where the stream widens and the water is not more than waist deep for the shortest member of your party. The tail end of an island is usually a good place as is a long riffle. The inside of a meander sometimes makes a safe ford, but in other cases a long, shallow section can be followed by a short, deep section next to the outside of the bend where the current picks up speed and carves out a deep channel.

Before starting any serious ford, make sure your matches, camera, billfold, clothes, sleeping bag, and other items that must be kept dry are in watertight bags.

In the Indian Peaks Wilderness, most streams are cold, so have dry clothes ready when you get to the other side to minimize the risk of hypothermia, especially on a cold, rainy day. Minimize the amount of time you spend in the water, but don't rush across. Instead, go slowly and deliberately, taking one step at a time, being careful to get each foot securely planted before lifting the other foot. Move at a 45-degree angle to the current instead of going straight across, following a riffle line if possible.

Don't ford with bare feet. Wear hiking boots without socks, sneakers, or tightly strapped sandals. In an emergency, wool socks pulled over rubber soles provide a good grip on the slippery rock.

When in mountainous terrain, and if you have a choice, ford in the early morning when the stream isn't as deep. The cool evening temperatures slow snow melt and reduce the water flow into the rivers.

On small streams, a sturdy walking stick used on the upstream side for balance helps prevent a fall, but in a major river with a fast current, a walking stick offers little help. Loosen the belt and straps on your pack. If you fall or get washed downstream, a waterlogged pack can anchor you to the bottom, so you must be able to easily release your pack.

If you're a strong swimmer, you might feel secure crossing a big river, but you might have children or smaller hikers in your party. In this case, the strongest person can cross first and string a line across the river to aid those who follow. This line (with the help of a carabiner) can also be used to float packs across instead of taking the chance that a waterlogged pack could drag you under. (If you know about the ford in advance, you can pack along a lightweight rubber raft or inner tube for this purpose.) Depending on size and strength, you might also want to carry children. In some cases, two or three people can cross together, locking forearms with the strongest person on the upstream side.

Be prepared for the worst. Sometimes circumstances arise where you simply must cross instead of going back, even though the ford looks dangerous. Also, you can underestimate the depth of the channel or strength of the current, especially after a thunderstorm when a muddy river hides its true depth. In these cases, whether you like it or not, you might be swimming.

If this happens, don't panic and do not try to swim directly across. Instead, pick a long angle and gradually cross to the other side, taking as much as a 100 yards or more to finally get across. If your pack starts to drag you down, release it immediately, even if you have to abandon it. If you lose control and get washed downstream, go feet first so you don't hit your head on rocks or logs.

Be sure to report any dangerous ford to a ranger as soon as you finish your trip.

Mountain Lions

You're sure to see plenty of deer or elk in the Indian Peaks Wilderness Area, which means mountain lions probably aren't far away. Cougars feed on deer, and the remote backcountry of this area constitutes some of the best cougar habitat in the West. Though many people consider themselves lucky indeed to see a mountain lion in the wild, the big cats—nature's perfect predator—are potentially dangerous. Attacks on humans are extremely rare, but it's wise to educate yourself before heading into mountain lion habitat.

To stay as safe as possible when hiking in mountain lion country, follow this advice:

- Travel with a friend or group and stay together.

- Don't let small children wander away by themselves.

- Don't let pets run unleashed.

- Avoid hiking at dawn and dusk—the times mountain lions are most active.

- Know how to behave if you encounter a mountain lion.

In the vast majority of mountain lion encounters, these animals exhibit avoidance, indifference, or curiosity and do not injure humans. However, if you have an encounter of any kind, try to keep your cool and consider the following:

- Recognize threatening mountain lion behavior. A few cues may help you gauge the risk of attack. If a mountain lion is more than 50 yards away and it directs its attention to you, it may be only curious. This situation represents only a slight risk for adults but a more serious risk to unaccompanied children. At this point, you should move away while keeping the animal in your peripheral vision. Also, look for rocks, sticks, or something to use as a weapon, just in case. If a mountain lion is crouched and staring at you less than 50 yards away, it may be assessing the chances of a successful attack. If this behavior continues, the risk of attack may be high.

- Do not approach a mountain lion. Give the animal the opportunity to move on. Slowly back away, but maintain eye contact if close. Mountain lions are not known to attack humans to defend young or a kill, but they have been reported to "charge" in rare instances and may want to remain in an area. If this is the case, it's best to choose another route or time to hike through an area.

- Do not run from a mountain lion. Running may stimulate a predatory response. If you encounter a mountain lion, be vocal and talk or yell loudly and regularly. Try not to panic. Shout to make others in the area aware of the situation. Maintain eye contact. Eye contact presents a challenge to the mountain lion, showing you are aware of its presence. Eye contact also helps you know where it is. However, if the behavior of the mountain lion is not threatening (if it is, for example, grooming or periodically looking away), maintain visual contact through your peripheral vision and move away.

- Appear larger than you are. Raise your arms above your head and make steady waving motions. Raise your jacket or another object above your head. Do not bend over, as this will make you appear smaller and more preylike.

- Pick up small children traveling with you. Bring the child close to you, maintain eye contact with the mountain lion, and pick the child up without bending over. If you are with other children or adults, band together.

- Defend yourself and others. If attacked, fight back. Try to remain standing. Do not feign death. Pick up a branch or rock; pull out a knife, pepper spray, or other deterrent device. Individuals have fended off mountain lions with rocks, tree limbs, and even cameras. Keep in mind that this is a last effort and defending pets is not recommended.

- Respect any warning signs posted by agencies.

- Teach others in your group how to behave in case of a mountain lion encounter.

- Report encounters. Record your location and the details of any encounter and notify the nearest land owner or land-managing agency. The land management agency (federal, state, or county) may want to visit the site and, if appropriate, post education/warning signs. Fish and wildlife agencies should also be notified because they record and track such encounters.

- Leave the area and do not disturb the site if an attack occurs. Mountain lions that have attacked people must be killed, and an undisturbed site is critical for effectively locating the dangerous mountain lion.

Bears

The first step to any hike in bear country is an attitude adjustment. Being prepared for bears doesn't only mean having the right equipment; it also means having the right information. The black bears found in the Indian Peaks Wilderness Area do not as a rule attack humans, but they may pose a danger if you handle your food improperly. At the very least, letting a bear get human food is like contributing—directly—to the eventual destruction of that bear. Think of proper bear etiquette as protecting the bears as much as yourself.

Staying overnight in bear country is not dangerous, but the presence of food, cooking, and garbage adds an additional risk to your trip. Plus, you are in bear country at night when bears are usually most active. To greatly minimize the chance of an encounter, follow a few basic guidelines:

- Store everything that has any food smell. Ziploc bags are perfect for reducing food smell and help keep food from spilling on your pack, clothing, or other gear. If you spill something on your clothes, change into other clothes for sleeping and hang clothes with food smells with the food and garbage. If you take them into the tent, you aren't separating your sleeping area from food smells. Try to keep food odors off your pack, but if you fail, put the food bag inside and hang the pack.

- Be sure to finalize your food-storage plans before it gets dark. It's not only difficult to store food after darkness falls, but it's easier to forget some juicy morsel on the ground. Store food in airtight, sturdy, waterproof bags to prevent food odors from circulating throughout the forest. You can purchase dry bags at most outdoor specialty stores, but you can get by with a trash-compactor bag. Don't use regular garbage bags as they can break too easily.

- See the diagrams below for different ways to hang a bear bag.

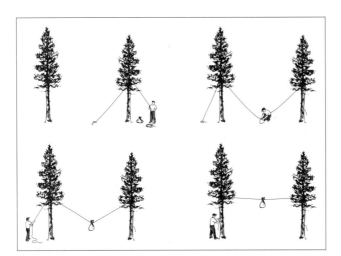

Hanging food and garbage between two trees.

Hanging food and garbage over a tree branch.

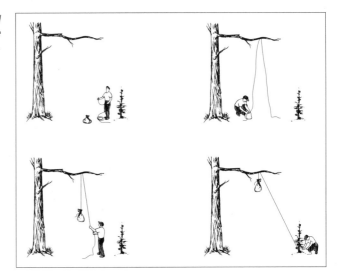

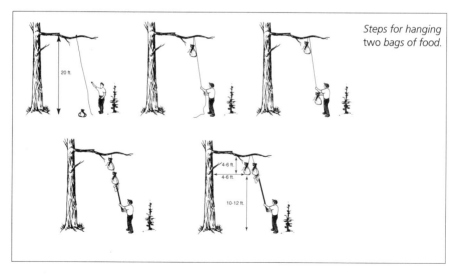

Hanging food and garbage over a leaning tree.

If you have *two* bags to hang, divide your food into two equal sacks. Use a stone to toss the end of a piece of nylon cord (parachute cord is fine; under most circumstances there is no need for the heavier stuff) over the limb well out from the trunk, then tie half your food to the end. Pull the food up to the limb, then tie your remaining food sack onto the cord as high as you can reach. Stuff the excess cord into the food sack, then use a stick to push the second sack several feet higher than your head. The first sack will act as a counterweight and descend a few feet, but it should remain at least as high as the second sack. In the morning, use a stick to pull down one of the sacks.

Steps for hanging two bags of food.

- Don't get paranoid about the types of food you bring—all food has some smell. By consciously reducing the number of dishes (pack out all food

13

scraps) and consuming everything on your plate, as well as paying careful attention to storage, you will not only make your backpacking culinary experience more enjoyable and hassle free for yourself, but also more bear proof.

Read *Bear Aware* by Bill Schneider for complete information on camping in bear country.

HIKING WITH CHILDREN

One of the greatest joys my wife and I have had is the time we have spent with our three children in the woods. Hiking is a wonderful sport that can be enjoyed by the entire family. With that said, things can go wrong with children when you are out in the woods, and they can go wrong real fast. Be prepared! Take extra clothing, food, diapers, water, and a healthy sense of humor.

Going on shorter hikes is the best way to introduce your child to the outdoors. Your child's age and fitness level will dictate how many miles you will travel in the woods. For toddlers a mile to 4 miles will be just right. Toddlers are the hardest to travel with in the woods, and, depending on how much or how long you want to carry them, your hike could be shorter. My son Jeremy had his own little backpack at the age of five, and he loved to carry his own food and water when we went into the woods. Older children travel at a faster rate and are strong enough to carry most of their gear. They require less attention and like to travel ahead of the adults exploring on their own. Make sure the older children don't travel too far ahead and emphasize that they stay on the trail and wait for you at all trail junctions.

Children are on a different agenda that most adults. They travel at a slower pace; they stop and check things out. Tree stumps, streams, butterflies, flowers, snow, and lakes are quite fascinating to their inquiring minds. They like to look at animals and bugs. They will stop and sit down for no reason at all. They will ask a million questions. Enjoy your time with your children. Stop and answer all those questions. You won't regret it.

HOW TO GET THERE

The Indian Peaks Wilderness Area is conveniently located near Colorado's Front Range and can be easily accessed from Colorado Springs, Denver, Boulder, and Fort Collins. For hikes in the eastern part of the wilderness, follow CO 119 (in Boulder) to the town of Nederland. From Nederland follow directions for your selected hike and proper trailhead.

For hikes in the western part of the wilderness, follow I-70 west from Denver to US 40. Travel north on US 40 over Berthoud Pass to Winter Park. Follow directions for your selected hike and proper trailhead.

SEASONS AND WEATHER

The hiking and backpacking season for the Indian Peaks Wilderness Area is limited to the months of May, June, July, August, September, and into late

October. Depending on elevation and snowfall, some trails will be covered in snow well into June. Other trails at lower elevations are free of the white stuff by early May.

Spring run-off in the month of June can be problem as small streams become swollen with raging snow melt from the higher elevations. Use caution and common sense when trying to cross any streams at these times. July is the month for blooming wildflowers—which are at their peak at this time and often quite spectacular—and sudden thunderstorms. Thunderstorms appear quite suddenly during the month of July and can be extremely violent. Plan on climbing any peak early in the morning and be off exposed ridges by noon or 1:00 P.M. at the latest.

Early August is a great time to explore the Indian Peaks Wilderness Area. The thunderstorms have usually passed by this time, and the streams have receded back to their normal levels. There are still many wildflowers, and the higher trails are free of snow. By late August the weather begins to change as temperatures drop. There is a noticeable change in the landscape as the higher elevations prepare for the onslaught of winter.

September usually is a time of stable weather and the changing of the aspens. The crowds of the summer have all but disappeared, and you can usually have your pick of campsites. By early October you can expect much cooler temperatures, and there is a good chance of snow. If you are traveling in the wilderness area at this time, be prepared for sudden weather changes and carry extra clothing.

The winter months are a time of heavy snowfalls and extreme low temperatures. Winter usually lasts from October to early June. If you are planning to travel in the wilderness at this time, be prepared. Winter in the Indian Peaks can be extremely harsh and unforgiving.

Snowshoeing on Forest Lakes Trail.

Using This Guide

Resting below Pawnee Pass.

In this book I describe thirty-eight hikes in and around the Indian Peaks Wilderness Area. These hikes vary from short (3 miles or less) day hikes to extended excursions that require up to three to four days in the backcountry. You will find **one-way hikes** that start at a trailhead and hike into a certain destination and return via the same trail. There are also **loop hikes** that use one or more trails to make a loop and return to the starting trailhead and **shuttle hikes** that begin and end at two different trailheads.

After you familiarize yourself with the area, you can mix and match hikes to suit your personal likes, time frame, and fitness level. Many of the hikes in this book are long day hikes or multiday excursions. Feel free to follow the trail description and hike as far as your mind and body will take you, enjoy the area, and then turn around and head back to the trailhead.

I have given each hike a **difficulty rating,** something that you should use as a reference point as to how hard a hike is going to be for you. What may be easy for some may turn out to be difficult for others. Physical conditioning, weather, trail conditions, and altitude all play roles in the rating of a trail or hike. Keep in mind that what feels easy at 8,000 feet becomes an all-out grunt at 13,000 feet. Some trails and hikes in the Indian Peaks Wilderness have smooth sections that within a short distance become rough, rocky, and steep. Some hikes are only 3 to 4 miles long but start at 10,000 feet and travel up to more than 13,000 feet. These hikes can be quite demanding and strenuous. Other hikes can be 8 miles long but travel on smooth, level trails and have little elevation gain. These hikes can be considerably easier. When planning your hike, take into consideration your level of fitness, your ability to function at higher altitudes, and your time frame.

The hikes in this guide are rated as easy, moderate, or strenuous. An **easy** hike is usually on a shorter hike or trail, with gentle grades and little elevation gain. **Moderate** hikes are longer but are usually less than 10 miles round-trip. Elevation gain can be between 1,000 and 2,000 feet. These hikes can be difficult for the beginning hiker. **Strenuous** hikes in this book have steep elevation gain, rocky or difficult trails, and high altitude. These hikes require a high fitness level, strong legs and lungs, proper equipment, and good map-reading skills.

For each hike in this guide there are **elevation graphs,** which show the rate of ascent or descent for a given trail, point of interest, or destination. Take into consideration that short climbs or drops will not appear on the elevation graph because of the small scale of the maps.

In this guide there is also a **location map,** which provides a general reference as to the location of your chosen hike.

Each hike in this guide is described in detail, including natural features, flowers, natural history, human history, lay of the land, and various other tidbits to make your hike more enjoyable.

Most of the trails in this guide have numbers associated with the trail name (e.g., Diamond Lake Trail is also known as FS 975). All of the hikes and trails are described by name, but the number is also mentioned when applicable.

Trails change, get rerouted, and are often closed for a number of reason, so keep this in mind as you use this guide. I have made every effort to be clear as to the difficulty and nature of each hike and trail in this guide, but it is up to you to be well informed, be prepared, be responsible for your own safety.

Author's Recommendations

Day Hikes	1 St. Vrain Mountain Trail
	2 Rock Creek Trail
	4 Lower Buchanan Pass Trail
	10 Ceran St. Vrain Trail
	13 Mount Audubon Trail
	14 Mitchell Lake Trail/Blue Lake Trail
	15 Lake Isabelle
	18 Niwot Ridge Trail
	20 Rainbow Lakes
	23 Arapaho Pass Trail to Lake Dorothy
	24 Diamond Lake
	25 Lost Lake
	32 Forest Lakes Trail
	37 Columbine Lake Trail
	38 Caribou Pass Trail
Family Hikes	4 Lower Buchanan Pass Trail
	10 Ceran St. Vrain Trail
	14 Mitchell Lake Trail/Blue Lake Trail
	15 Lake Isabelle
	16 Jean Luning Trail
	20 Rainbow Lakes
	31 Upper Forest Lakes
	37 Columbine Lake Trail
Wildflower Hikes	1 St. Vrain Mountain Trail
	2 Rock Creek Trail
	8 Coney Lake Trail
	14 Mitchell Lake Trail/Blue Lake Trail
	15 Lake Isabelle
	16 Jean Luning Trail
	18 Niwot Ridge Trail
	24 Diamond Lake
	25 Lost Lake
	27 Southern Loop
	29 King Lake Trail
	32 Forest Lakes Trail
	35 Cascade Creek Trail to Crater Lake
	37 Columbine Lake Trail
	38 Caribou Pass Trail
Peak Bagging	1 St. Vrain Mountain Trail
	5 Buchanan Pass Trail to Sawtooth Mountain
	11 South St. Vrain Trail
	13 Mount Audubon Trail
	21 Arapaho Glacier Trail
	23 Arapaho Pass Trail to Lake Dorothy

Peak Bagging (continued)	33 Heart Lake Trail to James Peak
	36 West Arapaho Pass Trail to Caribou Lake
	38 Caribou Pass Trail
Backcountry Excursions	5 Buchanan Pass Trail to Sawtooth Mountain
	7 St. Vrain Glacier Trail
	8 Coney Lake Trail
	9 North Loop
	24 Diamond Lake
	26 Devils Thumb Trail to Jasper Lake
	27 Southern Loop
	28 Woodland Lake Trail
	29 King Lake Trail
	33 Heart Lake Trail to James Peak
	34 Roaring Fork Trail
	35 Cascade Creek Trail to Crater Lake
	36 West Arapaho Pass Trail to Caribou Lake
	37 Columbine Lake Trail
	38 Caribou Pass Trail
Fishing Hikes	2 Rock Creek Trail
	7 St. Vrain Glacier Trail
	8 Coney Lake Trail
	10 Ceran St. Vrain Trail
	14 Mitchell Lake Trail/Blue Lake Trail
	15 Lake Isabelle
	20 Rainbow Lakes
	23 Arapaho Pass Trail to Lake Dorothy
	25 Lost Lake
	26 Devils Thumb Trail to Jasper Lake
	27 Southern Loop
	28 Woodland Lake Trail
	29 King Lake Trail
	31 Upper Forest Lakes
	32 Forest Lakes Trail
	33 Heart Lake Trail to James Peak
	34 Roaring Fork Trail
	35 Cascade Creek Trail to Crater Lake
	37 Columbine Lake Trail
Hikes for Photographers	1 St. Vrain Mountain Trail
	5 Buchanan Pass Trail to Sawtooth Mountain
	7 St. Vrain Glacier Trail
	8 Coney Lake Trail
	9 North Loop
	13 Mount Audubon Trail
	14 Mitchell Lake Trail/Blue Lake Trail

Hikes for Photographers (continued)	15 Lake Isabelle 17 Pawnee Pass Trail 21 Arapaho Glacier Trail 23 Arapaho Pass Trail to Lake Dorothy 24 Diamond Lake 27 Southern Loop 29 King Lake Trail 33 Heart Lake Trail to James Peak 34 Roaring Fork Trail 36 West Arapaho Pass Trail to Caribou Lake 37 Columbine Lake Trail 38 Caribou Pass Trail
Long, Hard Day Hikes	1 St. Vrain Mountain Trail 13 Mount Audubon Trail 17 Pawnee Pass Trail 21 Arapaho Glacier Trail 26 Devils Thumb Trail to Jasper Lake 32 Forest Lakes Trail 38 Caribou Pass Trail
Wildlife-Viewing Hikes	2 Rock Creek Trail 8 Coney Lake Trail 18 Niwot Ridge Trail 27 Southern Loop 30 Jenny Creek Trail 32 Forest Lakes Trail 33 Heart Lake Trail to James Peak 35 Cascade Creek Trail to Crater Lake 38 Caribou Pass Trail
Base-Camp Options	5 Buchanan Pass Trail to Sawtooth Mountain 8 Coney Lake Trail 26 Devils Thumb Trail to Jasper Lake 29 King Lake Trail 32 Forest Lakes Trail 33 Heart Lake Trail To James Peak 36 West Arapaho Pass Trail to Caribou Lake 38 Caribou Pass Trail

1 St. Vrain Mountain Trail

Highlights: This is one of the best hikes in the Indian Peaks Wilderness. The views out to the Wild Basin area of Rocky Mountain National Park, Longs Peak, and the Indian Peaks are nothing short of spectacular and make this a must-do hike in the Indian Peaks. The lower section of the trail follows along a wildly flowing creek and has some of the best wildflowers in the Indian Peaks.

Season: June to October.

Distance: 4.7 miles one-way.

Difficulty: Moderate to difficult.

Map: Trails Illustrated Indian Peaks/Gold Hill, #102.

Management: Boulder Ranger District, USDA Forest Service.

Trail conditions: The trail becomes narrow and rocky the higher you climb. Expect snow on the upper section of the trail well into June.

Finding the trailhead: From Boulder follow US 36 west to the town of Lyons. Take SR 7 north up to the small town of Allenspark. Go left on CR 107 (Ski Road) for 2.2 miles to St. Vrain Mountain Trailhead and parking.

Key points:

0.6   Wilderness boundary.
1.0   Branch of Rock Creek on the left.
3.0   Rocky Mountain National Park boundary.
4.0   Junction with the Rock Creek Trail.
4.5   Summit of St. Vrain Mountain.

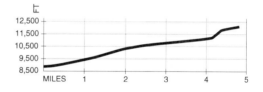

The hike: The hike starts at the St. Vrain Mountain Trailhead, 2 miles from the town of Allenspark. The trail begins at 8,800 feet and takes a gentle slope up through a beautiful forest of aspen and lodgepole pine. Wildflowers abound all along both sides of the trail as you enter the Indian Peaks Wilderness Area at the 0.6-mile mark. Once in the wilderness area the trail becomes narrow, rocky, and steeper.

At the 1-mile mark a branch of Rock Creek is on the left. This is a great place to stop and enjoy the spectacular array of wildflowers that grows in the moist area around the creek. Alpine sunflower, golden aster, golden banner, alpine avers, alpine daisy, mountain lupine, scarlet paintbrush, and alpine primrose grow profusely around the stream, and the bright, bold colors light up the hillsides. The trail switchbacks away from the stream and climbs steadily through a mixed conifer forest on its way to a saddle below Meadow Mountain. The trail climbs up though a twisted pine forest, following rock cairns into a saddle, alpine tundra, the Rocky Mountain National Park

St. Vrain Mountain Trail • Rock Creek Trail

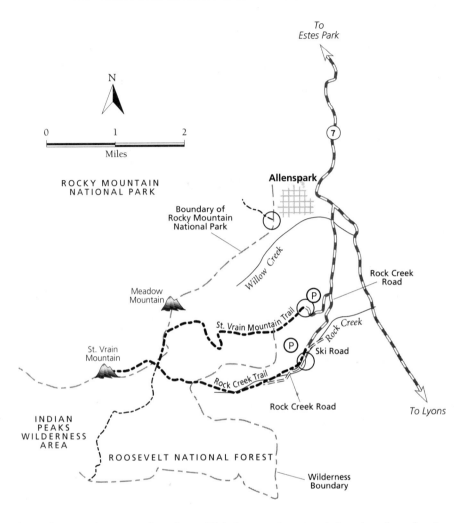

boundary, and spectacular views. This is a good spot to take a break and enjoy the views and mountain splendor.

At the Rocky Mountain National Park boundary, the trail cuts across the alpine tundra in a southerly direction toward St. Vrain Mountain. Be on the lookout for tiny alpine flowers that grow along both sides of the trail and the surrounding tundra. Reach a saddle around the 3.8-mile mark with views to the south, north, and east. Go right, following a vague trail and rock cairns for 0.7 mile, to the summit of St. Vrain Mountain.

Camping: Along the trail.

2 Rock Creek Trail

See Map on Page 22

Highlights: This is an adventurous hike up the steep slopes along beautiful Rock Creek. Wildflowers are abundant during the summer months, and Ski Road is great for ski touring or snowshoeing in the winter. Once you reach the junction with the St. Vrain Mountain Trail, the views out to the Wild Basin area of Rocky Mountain National Park, Longs Peak, and the Indian Peaks are nothing short of spectacular.

Season: May to October.

Distance: 3.5 miles one-way.

Difficulty: Moderate to difficult.

Map: Trails Illustrated Indian Peaks/Gold Hill, #102.

Management: Boulder Ranger District, USDA Forest Service.

Trail conditions: The lower section of the trail follows a four-wheel-drive road. The upper section of the trail along Rock Creek is hard to follow and all but disappears near the intersection with the St. Vrain Mountain Trail.

Finding the trailhead: From Boulder follow US 36 west to the town of Lyons. Take SR 7 north up to the small town of Allenspark. Go left on CR 107 (Ski Road) for 3.2 miles to a forest service kiosk and parking on the right. Most two-wheel-drive vehicles should have no problems negotiating the last mile to the kiosk.

Key points:

1.0 Go right across Rock Creek.

1.7 Go left over Rock Creek to Ski Road (CR 107).

2.8 Junction with St. Vrain Mountain Trail.

3.5 St. Vrain Mountain summit.

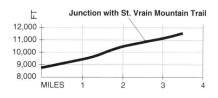

The hike: The hike starts near the site of the old Rock Creek Ski Area, which was established before World War II and was operated with a single towrope up the north slope of the steep hillside on the left side of Ski Road (CR 107). Follow the steep, rough jeep road uphill for roughly a mile to a road that goes right across Rock Creek. Cross over Rock Creek and go left up the steep forested slope with Rock Creek on your left. Ignore all side roads on the right and climb steeply up to where the trail goes left back across Rock Creek and back to Ski Road. Ski Road takes a sharp left; look to the right for a rock cairn and a trail leading up into the steep hillside. Follow the trail up for 0.3 mile and angle right across Rock Creek. The trail now follows along the right side of Rock Creek and climbs very steeply along the drainage. The wildflowers along the creek in the summer months are spectacular and are worth the effort of the climb.

Wildflowers along Rock Creek.

The crux of the hike is to find your way through the dense twisted pines up to the junction with the St. Vrain Mountain Trail. Stay left of Rock Creek and follow the overgrown trail up to the St. Vrain Mountain Trail. At the St. Vrain Mountain Trail go to the right up to a saddle and breathtaking views in all directions. At the saddle go left and climb for 0.7 mile to the summit of St. Vrain Mountain and panoramic views.

Bring a map and compass for this hike and remember to use St. Vrain Mountain as a reference point and landmark to reach the St. Vrain Mountain Trail.

Camping: Rock Creek Road.

3 Sourdough Trail North

Highlights: This is a wonderful hike into dense spruce forest with wildflowers, small streams, and occasional views to the high peaks. You can easily hook up with a number of excellent trails in the area to customize your hike to fit any ability. This is an excellent family hike.

Season: May to late October.

Distance: 6.1 miles one-way.

Difficulty: Moderate to strenuous.

Map: Trails Illustrated Indian Peaks/Gold Hill, #102.

Management: Boulder Ranger District, USDA Forest Service.

Trail conditions: The trail is popular with hikers and mountain cyclists as it is smooth in some sections and extremely rocky in others.

Finding the trailhead: From the intersection of Canyon and Broadway in Boulder, go west on Canyon (SR 119) for 16 miles to Nederland. Go right on SR 72 (Peak to Peak Highway) for 15 miles to the Camp Dick Campground turnoff. Turn left into Camp Dick and park at the South St. Vrain Trailhead on the left.

Key points:

0.3 Trail forks.

0.8 Trail junction.

1.9 Bridge.

2.3 Beaver Reservoir Road.

3.5 Junction with CR 96J.

3.7 Trail forks.

4.4 Junction with Wapiti-Baptisti Trail.

6.1 Junction with Wapiti-Baptisti Trail.

Junction with Wapiti-Baptiste Trail

10,000
9,500
9,000
8,500
8,000

MILES 1   2   3   4   5   6   7

The hike: The Sourdough Trail (FS 835) parallels the Peak to Peak Highway and stretches almost 18 miles from Rainbow Lakes Road at its most southern point to Peaceful Valley in the north. Along the way the trail connects with several trails around the Brainard Lake Recreation Area and the Peaceful Valley Campground. With the help of a map and compass you can connect with other trails for a variety of loops and distances, from short day hikes to multiday excursions. The best way to hike the Sourdough Trail is to arrange a car shuttle from the various trailheads. This eliminates any backtracking, and you can cover more territory. Determine your route and leave a car at each trailhead.

This hike is described going north to south, starting at Peaceful Valley and traveling south to Brainard Lake Road. The trail is quite popular with

Sourdough Trail North

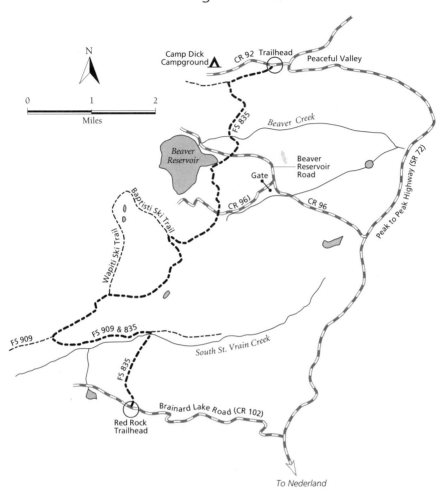

mountain bikers and trailrunners during the summer months, so be on the lookout for other trail users. The trail is an excellent ski or snowshoe tour during the winter months; it should be free of snow by late April or early May and stays green until late October or early November.

Your hike starts at the South St. Vrain Trailhead and follows that trail west to a junction with the Sourdough Trail (FS 835) in less than a mile of easy, level hiking. The Sourdough Trail goes left up a steep, rocky staircase to a ridge. The trail stays fairly level through the tall pines and then drops down on smooth tread to a bridge crossing at a little less than 2 miles of hiking. Be on the lookout for wildflowers in the moist soil along the stream. Colorado columbines and the dainty twinflower love the shady evergreen forest and the moist, fertile ground along the stream.

Past the bridge the trail bears right, then drops down to Beaver Reservoir Road. This is a good spot to turn around if you're running out of time or just want a short hike. Cross over Beaver Reservoir Road and follow the Sourdough Trail up into a recently (1988) burned area with many downed trees. The area is now being reclaimed by beautiful wildflowers and young aspen trees that should make for a beautiful fall hike in the years to come.

The trail drops down to CR 96J, crosses it, and then forks to the right at a trail junction. Climb up rocky tread to a junction with Wapiti-Baptiste Trail on the right. Continue straight on the Sourdough Trail, which travels up to a beautiful meadow with spectacular views and two ponds. The aspen trees surrounding the ponds are quite lovely in the early fall with their shimmering golden leaves. Follow the trail around the pond and in a short distance arrive at a junction with Wapiti-Baptiste Trail on the right. This is where the hike turns around.

Options: Feel free to keep following the Sourdough Trail up to the South St. Vrain Trail then to Brainard Lake Road, for added mileage.

Camping: At Camp Dick Campground or along the trail.

4 Lower Buchanan Pass Trail

Highlights: This is a nice day hike along beautiful Middle St. Vrain Creek. Waterfalls, wildflowers, and views are the main attractions of this hike.

Season: June to October.

Distance: 4 miles one-way.

Difficulty: Moderate.

Map: Trails Illustrated Indian Peaks/Gold Hill, #102.

Management: Boulder Ranger District, USDA Forest Service.

Trail conditions: The lower part of the trail is rocky and wet in some sections. The trail is well traveled and sees a fair amount of traffic during weekends in the summer months. Mountain bikes are allowed on this part of the Buchanan Pass Trail.

Finding the trailhead: From the intersection of Canyon and Broadway in Boulder, drive 16 miles on SR 119 to Nederland. Go north on CO 72 for 15 miles to Peaceful Valley. Turn left and travel 1.3 miles to a large parking area just past the Camp Dick Campground.

Key points:
  1.5 Timberline Falls.
  3.5 Great views to Sawtooth Mountain.
  4.0 Trail junction.

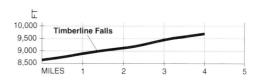

Lower Buchanan Pass Trail

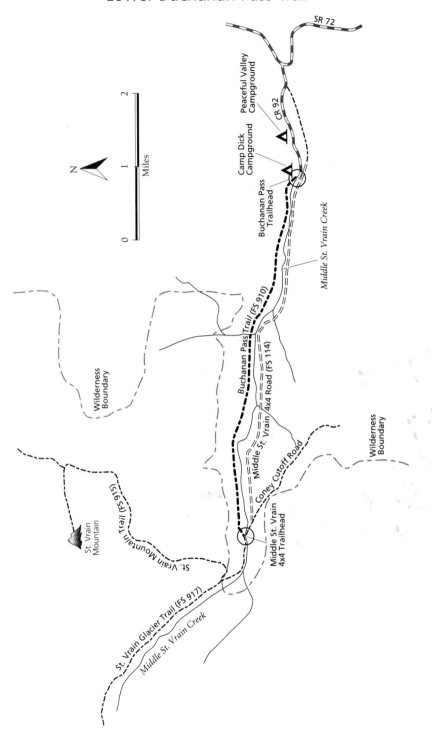

The hike: The hike starts at the parking area just west of the Camp Dick Campground. From the parking area go west on FS 114 for 100 feet to the Buchanan Pass Trail on the right. Cross the bridge over Middle St. Vrain Creek and follow the well-marked trail along the creek. This section of the trail is quite rocky and has little elevation gain. The trail takes a gentle grade up through a forest of aspen, lodgepole pine, and spruce trees up to Timberline Falls at the 1.5-mile mark. Wildflower lovers should be on the lookout for tall chiming bells, various paintbrushes, alpine daisies, black-eyed Susans, cow parsnips, and aspen sunflowers.

At the falls take a break and sit on the large boulders along the trail and enjoy the beauty of the tumbling waters. After the falls the trail climbs at a steeper grade up to an open meadow. At the meadow and the 2.8-mile mark the trail leaves the dense forest behind and spectacular views open up to the Indian Peaks. For the next mile the trail hugs the base of a steep hill with large boulders on the right side of the trail and Middle St. Vrain Creek on the left. At around the 3.8-mile mark the trail becomes quite narrow through an open meadow. This part of the trail remains muddy in even the driest years. Now you are only a short distance from your destination. The trail goes left toward Middle St. Vrain Creek, a bridge, FS 114, and the St. Vrain Glacier Trail.

Camping: At Camp Dick Campground and along the trail.

5 Buchanan Pass Trail to Sawtooth Mountain

Highlights:	This fantastic excursion up to Buchanan Pass and Sawtooth Mountain features alpine wildflowers, meadows, spectacular views, great camping sites, and an ascent of Sawtooth Mountain. This is a beautiful two- to three-day hike.
Season:	June to October.
Distance:	9.7 miles one-way.
Difficulty:	Moderate to strenuous.
Map:	Trails Illustrated Indian Peaks/Gold Hill, #102.
Management:	Boulder Ranger District, USDA Forest Service.
Trail conditions:	The lower part of the trail is rocky and wet in some sections. The trail is well traveled and sees a fair amount of traffic during weekends in the summer months. Mountain bikes are allowed on this part of the Buchanan Pass Trail. The upper part of the trail near Buchanan Pass holds snow well into the summer months.

Finding the trailhead: From the intersection of Canyon and Broadway in Boulder, drive 16 miles on SR 119 to Nederland. Go north on SR 72 for 15

Buchanan Pass Trail to Sawtooth Mountain

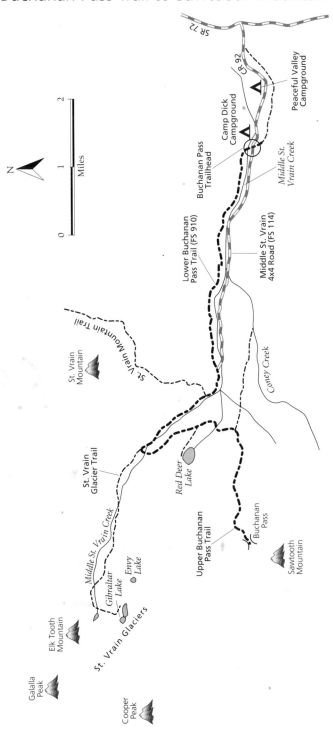

N

0 1 2
Miles

SR 72

CR 92

Peaceful Valley Campground

Camp Dick Campground

Buchanan Pass Trailhead

Middle St. Vrain Creek

Lower Buchanan Pass Trail (FS 910)

Middle St. Vrain 4x4 Road (FS 114)

Coney Creek

St. Vrain Mountain Trail

St. Vrain Mountain

St. Vrain Glacier Trail

Red Deer Lake

Upper Buchanan Pass Trail

Buchanan Pass

Sawtooth Mountain

Middle St. Vrain Creek

Gibraltar Lake

Envy Lake

St. Vrain Glaciers

Elk Tooth Mountain

Galalla Peak

Cooper Peak

miles to Peaceful Valley. Turn left and travel 1.3 miles to a large parking area just beyond the Camp Dick Campground.

Key points:
- 1.5   Timberline Falls.
- 3.5   Great views to Sawtooth Mountain.
- 4.0   Trail junction.
- 4.7   St. Vrain Mountain Trail.
- 5.5   Junction with St. Vrain Glacier Trail.
- 6.5   Red Deer Cutoff Trail.
- 7.3   Beaver Creek Trail.
- 9.3   Buchanan Pass.
- 9.7   Sawtooth Mountain.

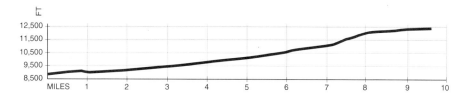

The hike: The hike starts at the parking area just west of Camp Dick Campground. From the parking area go west on FS 114 for 100 feet to the Buchanan Pass Trail on the right. Cross the bridge over St. Vrain Creek and follow the well-marked trail along the creek. This section of the trail is quite rocky and has little elevation gain. The trail takes a gentle grade up through a forest of aspen, lodgepole pine, and spruce trees up to Timberline Falls at the 1.5-mile mark. Wildflower lovers should be on the lookout for tall chiming bells, various paintbrushes, alpine daisies, black-eyed Susans, cow parsnips, and aspen sunflowers.

At the falls take a break, sit on the large boulders along the trail, and enjoy the beauty of the tumbling waters of St. Vrain Creek. After the falls the trail climbs at a steeper grade to an open meadow. At the meadow and the 2.8-mile mark the trail leaves the dense spruce forest behind, and spectacular views open up to the Indian Peaks. For the next mile the trail contours around the side of a steep hill with large boulders on the right side of the trail and St. Vrain Creek on the left. At around the 3.8-mile mark the trail becomes quite narrow through an open meadow. This part of the trail remains muddy in even the driest years. The trail goes left toward St. Vrain Creek, a bridge, FS 114, and the St. Vrain Glacier Trail. At the bridge continue west toward the mountains and up into a beautiful meadow along St. Vrain Creek. This is an excellent spot to set up camp and explore the trails in this part of the wilderness area.

Follow the trail up into the wilderness area and the St. Vrain Mountain Trail on the right. Continue straight into a wide-open meadow (another great spot to camp) to a trail junction at a bridge. Go left over the bridge that contours around a hill to the Red Deer Cutoff Trail on the right. If you have time, go right and up the steep, rocky trail for a little more than 0.5 mile to

Red Deer Lake. Camping is allowed at the lake, and the fishing is good for brook and brown trout.

Continue straight on the Buchanan Pass Trail to the Beaver Creek Trail on the left. Turn right at the trail junction and cross over several small streams, keeping the main creek on your left. Within a mile of nice hiking the landscape changes into alpine tundra and krummholz trees. The trail cuts through a small alpine meadow and then climbs up several switchbacks to Buchanan Pass. The snowfields last well into the summer months, and gaiters are useful. At the top of the pass take a short break, enjoy the spectacular views, and rest a little before climbing Sawtooth Mountain. The climb to Sawtooth Mountain goes left and climbs the ridge for a short, 0.5-mile hike to the summit. Reaching the summit requires no technical skills, so go for it and reap the rewards of impressive views in all directions.

You can continue on beyond Buchanan Pass, going west into a deep valley down to Cascade Creek and a junction with the Cascade Creek Trail. This trail leads to the Monarch Lake Trailhead and a spectacular 18-mile trek across the northern section of the wilderness area. This option requires a car shuttle and planning. Better yet, have someone pick you up at the Monarch Lake Trailhead with some refreshments.

Camping: At Camp Dick Campground, Peaceful Valley Campground, and along the trail.

Camping in the great outdoors.

6 St. Vrain Mountain Trail South

Highlights:	This great hike up to the summit of St. Vrain Mountain starts on the south side of St. Vrain Mountain off the Buchanan Pass Trail. Great views out to Mount Audubon, Paiute Peak, and the St. Vrain drainage make for a must-do hike in this part of the wilderness area. Wildflowers cover the hillsides on the lower part of the trail, and old-growth pines shoot up to the sky on the eastern flank of St. Vrain Mountain. You can access this part of the St. Vrain Mountain Trail by hiking the lower part of the Buchanan Pass Trail up to the Middle St. Vrain Trailhead. This makes a great two- to three-day hike, with excellent campsites located along the Middle St. Vrain just past the trailhead. The views from the summit of St. Vrain Mountain are incredible and extend in all directions.
Season:	June to October.
Distance:	4.5 miles one-way.
Difficulty:	Moderate to difficult.
Map:	Trails Illustrated Indian Peaks/Gold Hill, #102.
Management:	Boulder Ranger District, USDA Forest Service.
Trail conditions:	The trail becomes narrow and rocky the higher you climb. Expect snow on the upper sections of the trail well into June.

Finding the trailhead: From the intersection of Canyon and Broadway in Boulder, drive 16 miles on SR 119 to Nederland. Go north on CO 72 for 15 miles to Peaceful Valley. Turn left into the Camp Dick Campground. Follow FS114 (a rough, four-wheel drive road) for 4 miles to the trailhead, or hike the lower Buchanan Pass Trail (hike #4) to the trailhead.

Key points:

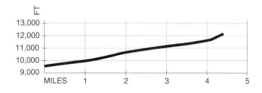

- 0.5 Wilderness boundary
- 0.6 St. Vrain Mountain Trail. Go right up the narrow, rocky trail.
- 1.0 Great views. Be on the lookout for wildflowers.
- 2.5 The trail levels out and drops down to a stream crossing.
- 3.5 Stream crossing. Continue straight up to a saddle.
- 4.0 Go left up to the summit of St. Vrain Mountain.
- 4.5 Summit of St. Vrain Mountain.

The hike: The hike starts at the Middle St. Vrain Trailhead, located 4 miles up the Buchanan Pass Trail. The first sections of the trial follows the Middle St. Vrain drainage on a well-marked path up to the Indian Peaks Wilderness boundary. There are numerous campsites along this portion of the

St. Vrain Mountain Trail South

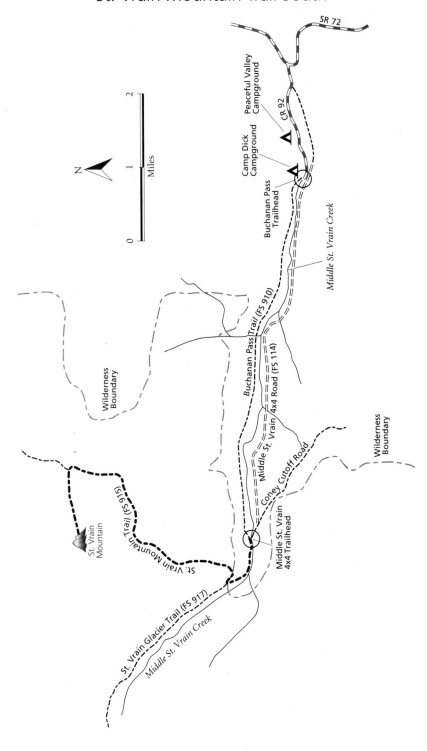

SR 72

Peaceful Valley Campground

CR 92

Camp Dick Campground

Buchanan Pass Trailhead

Middle St. Vrain Creek

N

Miles

0   1   2

Buchanan Pass Trail (FS 910)

Middle St. Vrain 4x4 Road (FS 114)

Wilderness Boundary

Coney Cutoff Road

Wilderness Boundary

St. Vrain Mountain Trail (FS 915)

St. Vrain Mountain

St. Vrain Glacier Trail (FS 917)

Middle St. Vrain 4x4 Trailhead

Middle St. Vrain Creek

trail, which also makes for an excellent base camp for exploring the other trails in the area. Just past the wilderness boundary, look for the St. Vrain Mountain Trail on the right. This begins the start of steep hiking as you gain more than 1,500 feet in a little less than 2 miles. The views west and south to Mount Audubon and Sawtooth Mountain are just beautiful and keep your mind off the strenuous hiking and your tired legs.

Wildflowers grow along the several drainages that you will pass by along this section of the trail. Once you gain the ridge the trail levels out and becomes quite pleasant as you lose some elevation traversing along the base of St. Vrain Mountain. Continue straight through a forest of tall pine trees across a small stream up to an obvious saddle just below the summit of St. Vrain Mountain. Go left, following a faint trail up through the scree to the summit. Take a well-deserved break and enjoy the spectacular views to Rocky Mountain National Park, the eastern plains, and the Indian Peaks. Turn around and retrace your route back to the trailhead.

If you plan to climb St. Vrain Mountain, give yourself enough time to complete the climb and try to be off the summit by noontime. The summit is exposed to the elements, and summer thunderstorms can be extremely violent.

Camping: At the trailhead and along the trail.

7 St. Vrain Glacier Trail

Highlights:	This great two-day backpack ventures into what was once a huge glacier valley. Wildflowers, waterfalls, towering rock walls, alpine lakes, and awesome views to Sawtooth and Elk Tooth Mountains are the main attractions of this hike.
Season:	June to October.
Distance:	8.2 miles one-way.
Difficulty:	Moderate to difficult.
Map:	Trails Illustrated Indian Peaks/Gold Hill, #102.
Management:	Boulder Ranger District, USDA Forest Service.
Trail conditions:	The lower part of the trail is rocky in some sections. The trail is well traveled and sees a fair amount of traffic during weekends in the summer months. The last 0.25 mile of the trail to Lake Gibraltar is almost nonexistent, and you will have to negotiate a large talus field up to the lake.

Finding the trailhead: From the intersection of Canyon and Broadway in Boulder, drive 16 miles on SR 119 to Nederland. Go north on SR 72 for 15 miles to Peaceful Valley. Turn left and travel 1.3 miles to a large parking area just past the Camp Dick Campground.

St. Vrain Glacier Trail

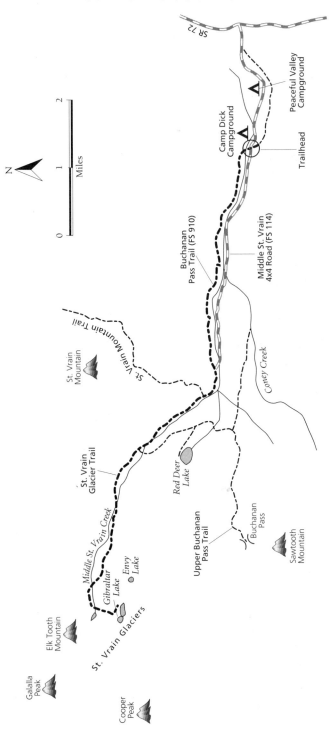

N

Miles

0   1   2

SR 72

Peaceful Valley Campground

Camp Dick Campground

Trailhead

Buchanan Pass Trail (FS 910)

Middle St. Vrain 4x4 Road (FS 114)

Coney Creek

St. Vrain Mountain Trail

St. Vrain Mountain

St. Vrain Glacier Trail

Red Deer Lake

Upper Buchanan Pass Trail

Buchanan Pass

Sawtooth Mountain

Middle St. Vrain Creek

Gibraltar Lake

Envy Lake

St. Vrain Glaciers

Elk Tooth Mountain

Galalla Peak

Cooper Peak

Key points:

    1.5   Timberline Falls.
    4.0   Trail junction.
    4.5   Indian Peaks Wilderness boundary.
    4.6   Junction with the St. Vrain Mountain Trail.
    5.6   Junction with the Buchanan Pass and Red Deer Lake Trails.
    6.6   Cross St. Vrain Creek at pond.
    8.2   Arrive at Lake Gibraltar.

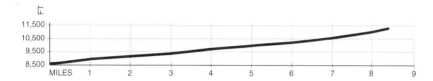

The hike: The hike starts at the parking area just west of the Camp Dick Campground. From the parking area go west on FS 114 for 100 feet to the Buchanan Pass Trail on the right. Cross the bridge over St. Vrain Creek and follow the well-marked trail along the creek. The trail takes a gentle grade up through a forest of aspen, lodgepole pine, and spruce trees up to Timberline Falls at the 1.5-mile mark. This is a great place to sit on the large boulders along the trail and enjoy the beauty of the tumbling waters of the falls.

At the 2.8-mile mark the trail leaves the dense forest behind, and gorgeous views open up to the Indian Peaks. The trail becomes very rocky and climbs up to a trail junction at a bridge, FS 114, and the St. Vrain Glacier Trail. Don't cross the bridge; continue straight up the rocky trail along Middle St. Vrain Creek. Various wildflowers grow in the wet areas along the trail, and Indian paintbrush seems to be the most common flower along the trail.

Hikers on the upper section of the St. Vrain Glacier Trail.

At the 4.5-mile mark you arrive at a large meadow and the boundary of the Indian Peaks Wilderness. At the upper west end of the meadow the St. Vrain Mountain Trail goes steeply up to St. Vrain Mountain on the right. Continue straight for a mile on the wide trail up to a large meadow filled with wildflowers and standing dead trees. At the upper end of the meadow the Buchanan Pass and the Red Deer Lake Trails make a sharp left over the bridge. Bear to the right on what is now the St. Vrain Glacier Trail. The trail begins to climb away from the creek and follows a narrow meadow of wildflowers and spruce trees. A section of the trail cuts through a beautiful meadow with some of the largest stands of cow parsnip I have ever seen.

Looking due west, rocky Elk Tooth Mountain (12,848 feet) looms high in the skyline, pulling you ever closer to the Continental Divide. The trail becomes quite narrow through a wet section and drops down to Middle St. Vrain Creek. Go left across the creek on a log bridge and follow the trail on the south side of the creek. Continue up the wide path to another creek crossing. The trail becomes narrow again and crosses the creek at a major log dam, which has created a small pond that is 3 to 5 feet deep and sits in a beautiful position in a large open meadow.

The trail continues up the valley with a pretty meadow on the right and a cascading waterfall on the left. The meadow on the right is a wonderful spot to set up camp for the night. Past the meadow, the trail climbs steeply on a narrow path that crosses several small streams and has impressive views of Elk Tooth Mountain and the surrounding cirque. The trail climbs up through a stand of twisted pines of the krummholtz zone and a boulder field with rock cairns pointing the way. The trail all but disappears at a large rock cairn, and the surrounding terrain becomes very alpine with tundra grasses and rocks. Pick a line up through the boulders near the creek, heading up to a small ridge. Gibraltar Lake lies just beyond the ridge below the towering glacier. There are no good camping spots near the lake; your best bet is to set up camp near the large rock cairn.

Camping: At Camp Dick Campground, Peaceful Valley Campground, and along the trail.

8 Coney Lake Trail

Highlights:	This nice two-day backpack leads up to a beautiful alpine lake surrounded by high peaks and steep talus slopes. Wildflowers grow all along Coney Creek, and Sawtooth Mountain dominates the skyline near Coney Flats.
Season:	June to October.
Distance:	5.9 miles one-way.
Difficulty:	Strenuous.
Map:	Trails Illustrated Indian Peaks/Gold Hill, #102.
Management:	Boulder Ranger District, Sulphur Ranger District, and USDA Forest Service.
Trail conditions:	Conditions vary from smooth, soft tread to rock-infested boulder fields on this hike.

Finding the trailhead: From the junction of SR 93 and SR 119 in Boulder, go west on SR 119 for 16 miles to Nederland. Go west on SR 72 for 12.5 miles to CR 96. Turn left on CR 96 for 2.5 miles to Beaver Reservoir and the trailhead on the right. You can eliminate walking the first 4 miles of the hike by driving to the Coney Flats Trailhead/Beaver Creek Trailhead; however, the road is extremely rough, and there can be washouts in several sections. Having a four-wheel-drive, high-clearance vehicle is a must. The mileage starts from the Coney Flats Trailhead/Beaver Creek Trailhead.

Key points:

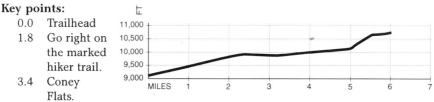

- 0.0 Trailhead
- 1.8 Go right on the marked hiker trail.
- 3.4 Coney Flats.
- 3.6 Coney Lake Trail.
- 4.3 Cross over Coney Creek on log bridge.
- 5.9 Arrive at lower Coney Lake.

The hike: The hike begins at the Coney Flats Trailhead/Beaver Creek Trailhead and follows the rough, rocky road through a dense spruce forest. Stay right at all intersections and be aware of ATV and four-wheel-drive traffic. At around the 1.8-mile mark the road takes a sharp left up a steep hill. Continue straight on the well-marked hiker and ski trail. The trail passes through several sections of private property and by several small ponds, becoming very rocky as you climb and then drop down to the ponds. The area near the ponds is often wet, and there are some log bridges to get you over the wet sections.

Past the ponds, the trail climbs on rocky tread back up to Coney Flats Road. Follow the road for 0.5 mile to Coney Flats. At Coney Flats the view of Sawtooth Mountain is just spectacular; the peak is one of the more impressive mountains in the wilderness area.

Coney Lake Trail

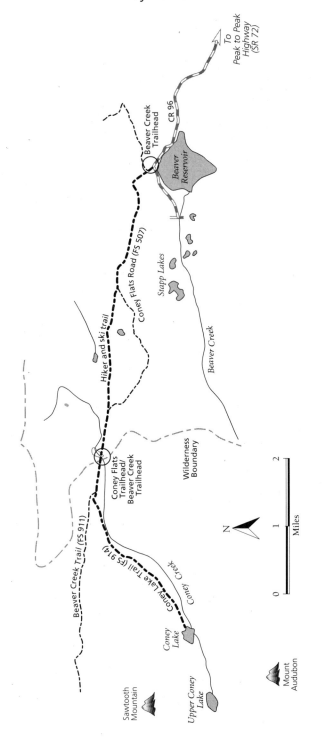

Wildflowers near Coney Flats.

Continue straight over several wooden bridges to the Coney Flats Trail-head. Go left on the Beaver Creek Trail for 0.2 mile to a junction with the Coney Lake Trail. Turn left on the Coney Creek Trail into an open meadow along Coney Creek. Wildflowers grow profusely along the trail and during the summer months the colors are sensational. Aspen daisy, scarlet paint-brush, cow parsnip, northern paintbrush, and snow buttercup are some of the more common flowers found along this section of the trail.

Cross over Coney Creek and follow the trail up what look to be remnants of an old logging road. The trail is steep, somewhat rocky, and climbs up to a level area where you forge over Coney Creek once again on a log bridge. The trail then winds through a meadow with several small ponds. This is a nice spot to take a short break before the climb up to Coney Lake. Go right around the largest of the ponds, climbing up through an often-wet area to a saddle. Power up and over the saddle and cruise down to Coney Lake. Coney Lake sits in an impressive position below the towering peaks of Sawtooth Mountain (12,304 feet) to the north and west, Paiute Peak (13,088 feet) to the west, and Mount Audubon (13,233 feet) to the south.

Upper Coney Lake is a mile west of Coney Lake. There is no trail up to Upper Coney Lake, but if you do decide to travel there, stay close to Coney Creek.

Camping: At Coney Flats and Coney Lake. Campsites are limited at the lake, and campfires are prohibited.

9 North Loop

Highlights:	This incredible, three- to four-day backcountry excursion in the northern section of the Indian Peaks Wilderness Area has views, wildflowers, alpine meadows, a waterfall, high mountain passes, and beautiful alpine lakes. This hike has it all.
Season:	Late June to early October.
Distance:	23.7-mile loop.
Difficulty:	Strenuous.
Map:	Trails Illustrated Indian Peaks/Gold Hill, #102.
Management:	Boulder Ranger District, Sulphur Ranger District, and USDA Forest Service.
Trail conditions:	Conditions vary from smooth, soft tread to rock-infested boulder fields and steep switchbacks.

Finding the trailhead: From the intersection of Broadway and Canyon in Boulder, go west on SR 119 for 16 miles to Nederland. Go west on SR 72 for 12.5 miles to CR 96. Go left on CR 96 for 2.5 miles to Beaver Reservoir and the trailhead on the right. Feel free to drive the 4 rough, rocky miles to the Coney Flats Trailhead/Beaver Creek Trailhead. The road is extremely rough, and there may be washouts in several sections. A four-wheel-drive, high-clearance vehicle is a must. The mileage starts from the Coney Flats Trailhead/Beaver Creek Trailhead.

Key points:
- 1.6   Buchanan Pass Trail (FS 910).
- 3.8   Buchanan Pass.
- 7.4   Gourd Lake Trail.
- 8.9   Cascade Creek Trail.
- 11.6   Pawnee Pass Trail.
- 13.0   Pawnee Lake.
- 14.5   Pawnee Pass.
- 17.0   Lake Isabelle.
- 19.0   Long Lake Trailhead.
- 23.7   Coney Flats Trailhead.

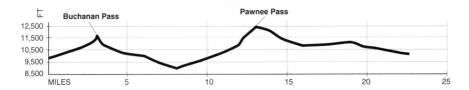

The hike: This is the big daddy of the multiday backcountry trips in the Indian Peaks, and it requires a high fitness level, proper equipment, and good map-reading skills. So what are you going to get for all your hard work? Spectacular alpine vistas, wildflowers, excellent backcountry camping, and an extraordinary tour of the northern Indian Peaks Wilderness Area.

North Loop

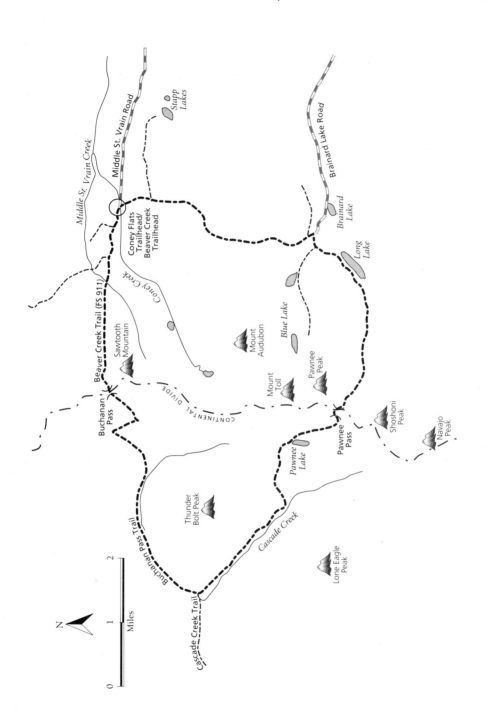

The hike starts at the Coney Flats Trailhead and travels west up to Buchanan Pass (11,837 feet). It then drops down into the Cascade Creek drainage on the Cascade Creek Trail to the Pawnee Pass Trail. The hike then follows the Pawnee Pass Trail up over Pawnee Pass (12,541 feet, the highest in the Indian Peaks) and down to Lake Isabelle and out to the upper Brainard Lake parking area. From the parking area the trail follows the Beaver Creek Trail up toward Mount Audubon, then north back to your starting point at the Coney Flats Trailhead.

Follow the well-marked Beaver Creek Trail across several wooden bridges up to the Coney Lake Trail (FS 914). Continue straight on the Beaver Creek Trail (FS 911), which has spectacular views of Sawtooth Mountain straight ahead and Mount Audubon to the left. After crossing over several small streams the trail travels up to Buchanan Pass Trail. The Beaver Creek Trail terminates at the junction with Buchanan Pass Trail. You now follow the Buchanan Pass Trail up toward Buchanan Pass through flower-filled meadows and several streams. Within a mile of nice hiking the landscape changes into alpine tundra and krummholz trees. The trail cuts through a small alpine meadow (with good camping sites) and then climbs up several switchbacks to Buchanan Pass. The snowfields last well into the summer months, and gaiters are useful when trekking through the wet, melting snow. At the top of the pass take a well-deserved rest before the steep descent down Buchanan Pass.

Buchanan Pass was once used as a stage road in the late 1800s, and through the years roads and railroads were planned for an east-to-west route over this part of the Continental Divide. As late as 1967 a toll road and a tunnel were planned. Thankfully these plans never came to fruition, and the area around the pass remains pristine. The pass was also used as a hunting ground by Native Americans as far back as 5000 B.C. Many hunting blinds and stone walls have been identified high in the tundra on Buchanan Pass, and ancient stone points have been found in the tundra grasses.

When you are rested, drop steeply down the pass and begin an enjoyable trek through dense spruce forest to the Gourd Lake Trailhead. The Gourd Lake Trail travels almost 3 miles up steep terrain to picturesque Gourd Lake. Go for it if you have the time. The lake is stocked with cutthroat trout and also has a number of excellent camping sites.

Continue straight down the Buchanan Pass Trail through lodgepole and spruce forests for 1.5 miles to a junction with the Cascade Creek Trail. You have now lost almost 3,000 feet of elevation that you fought so hard for on the east side of the pass. Go left on the Cascade Creek Trail, crossing over Cascade Creek and climbing up to Cascade Falls. Past the falls the trail stays on the east side of Cascade Creek up to Pawnee Pass Trail. Thunderbolt Peak (11,938 feet) and an unnamed peak (12,113 feet) can be seen high in the skyline to the east.

The trail now travels through an area of wet meadows with many water-loving alpine flowers dotting the landscape. Before you know it, you're at a junction with the Pawnee and Crater Lake Trails. Go left and begin a steady climb up to Pawnee Lake, a beautiful alpine lake set in a narrow valley below Pawnee Peak (12,943 feet) and Pawnee Pass (12,541 feet). There are great camping sites near the lake, and this is a good place to stop and rest before the grunt up and over to Pawnee Pass.

From the lake the trail goes through beautiful flower-filled meadows and then begins a steep, rocky ascent to Pawnee Pass via numerous tight switchbacks (more than twenty) up to 12,541 feet and Pawnee Pass. Take a break and enjoy the breathtaking views of the towering summit of Shoshoni Peak (12,967 feet), Navaho Peak (13,409 feet), Arikaree Peak (13,441 feet), and Pawnee Peak (12,943 feet). Drop steeply down the east side of Pawnee Pass to a shelf in open tundra. From this point the trail makes a dramatic drop down to Lake Isabelle via a number of rocky switchbacks through steep rock walls. The views of Lake Isabelle are stunning. Beautiful waterfalls tumble down near the lake and trail. The wildflowers along this section of the trail and near the lake are sensational, and it is worth an hour's stop.

From the lake to the parking area, the trail stays fairly level and contours around the north shore of Long Lake. At the parking area go north to the Coney Flats Trailhead, following Beaver Creek Trail up through a beautiful spruce forest to a junction with Mount Audubon Trail. Go right, staying on the Beaver Creek Trail, and travel through spectacular tundra. The trail crosses over Beaver Creek, hugs the boundary of the Indian Peaks Wilderness Area, and makes a steep drop through the trees to the Coney Flats Trailhead and your destination.

Camping: At Coney Flats and along the trail.

10 Ceran St. Vrain Trail

Highlights:	This beautiful trail through lodgepole pines along the St. Vrain Creek makes for an excellent family hike with good campsites, fishing, and access.
Season:	April to November.
Distance:	3.1 miles one-way.
Difficulty:	Moderate.
Map:	Trails Illustrated Indian Peaks/Gold Hill, #102.
Management:	Boulder Ranger District, USDA Forest Service.
Trail conditions:	The trail is smooth along the river and rocky near Miller Rocks.

Finding the trailhead: From Broadway and Canyon in Boulder, go north on Broadway for 4 miles to Lee Hill Road on the left. Take Lee Hill Road to Old Stage Road. Follow Old Stage Road for 4 miles to Lefthand Canyon Road. Turn left on Lefthand Canyon to Jamestown. Travel 4.7 miles past Jamestown to the turnoff for the trailhead. Go right into the parking area and trailhead.

Ceran St. Vrain Trail

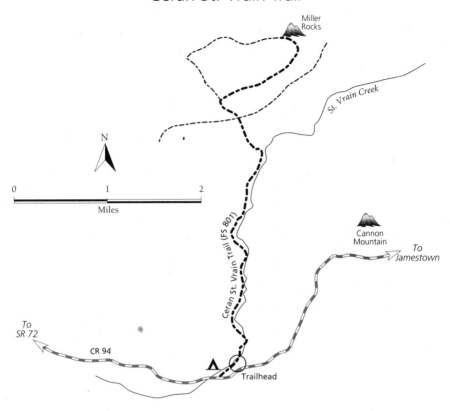

Key points:
- 1.9 Go left and up.
- 2.1 Trail junction at top of the hill. Go left and up.
- 2.4 Trail junction. Go right.
- 2.7 Go left.
- 3.1 Miller Rocks on the right.

The hike: The trailhead starts at the bridge over the St. Vrain Creek and guides you into a beautiful forest of lodgepole pines and wildflowers. This section of the trail is popular with campers and anglers and can be very crowded on weekend days during the summer months. The area near the trailhead and by the smooth water-worn rocks in the river is an excellent spot to hang out, eat some lunch, and enjoy the tumbling waters of the St. Vrain Creek. The trail climbs a short distance, then becomes quite narrow with steep drop-offs to the right. Be on the lookout for wildflowers and clusters of beautiful fairy slipper orchids during the early summer months. The fairy slipper is a rare flower of the orchid family that grows in the moist, shady evergreen forest of the Rocky Mountain foothills and in montane and subalpine ecosystems from Alaska in the north to New Mexico in the south.

The trail then pulls away from the river and makes a healthy descent to a trail junction at the 1.9-mile mark. Go left and up away from the river to a trail junction at the top of the hill. Go left again, up to another trail junction. The hike goes right on a narrow trail up to junction with an old logging road. Go left and up the road to Miller Rocks on the right. There is a trail around the base of the rocks, and an easy scramble leads to the top of the rocks, revealing spectacular views west to the Indian Peaks.

Ceran St. Vrain, guide, explorer, fur trader, and fort builder, played an important role in the settling of the wilderness now known as northern Colorado. With his partner, Charles Bent, he founded and built several forts in northern Colorado, with Fort St. Vrain, located at the confluence of the South Platte and St. Vrain Rivers the most famous. He was active in politics, business, and military affairs, and his name will be forever intertwined with the early history and settlement of northern Colorado.

Camping: At the trailhead, along the river, and near Miller Rocks.

11 South St. Vrain Trail

Highlights:	This wonderful day hike connects several trails along the St. Vrain drainage. A car shuttle is a good idea and makes for a more pleasant experience. Park one car at the South St. Vrain Trailhead and the other at the Mitchell Lake Trailhead north of Brainard Lake.
Season:	March to November.
Distance:	6.2 miles one-way.
Difficulty:	Easy to moderate.
Map:	Trails Illustrated Indian Peaks/Gold Hill, #102.
Management:	Boulder Ranger District, USDA Forest Service.
Trail conditions:	The trail varies from very smooth to extremely rocky.

Finding the trailhead: From the intersection of Canyon and Broadway in Boulder go west on Canyon (SR 119) 16 miles to Nederland. Go right on SR 72 (Peak to Peak Highway) and travel 11 miles to CR 96. Go left over CR 96, cross over a bridge, and park at the South St. Vrain Trailhead. The hike starts here.

Key points:
- 2.0 Baptist Road.
- 2.5 Trail junction.
- 2.7 Bridge.

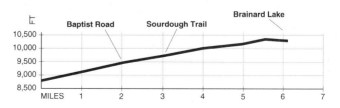

South St. Vrain Trail

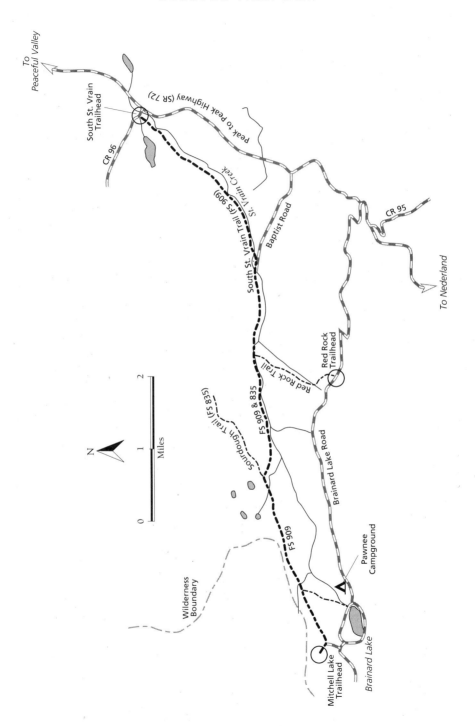

3.0   Trail junction.
5.3   Trail junction.
6.2   Brainard Lake Road.

The hike: The first 2 miles of the trail parallel the beautiful St. Vrain Creek and make an excellent short family hike to Baptist Road. Beyond Baptist Road the trail wanders through dense spruce forests and connects with many spur trails in and around the Brainard Lake Recreation Area. Bring a map and feel free to explore.

The first part of the trail stays close to the St. Vrain Creek and is an excellent place to see wildflowers during the early summer months. The trail is very narrow and can be rocky in certain sections. You gain almost 700 feet in the first 2 miles to Baptist Road, and along the way you travel through beautiful forests of aspen and spruce trees. Wildflowers grow along the creek and in the small open meadows, with paintbrush being the most common flower.

Once on Baptist Road, continue straight up to a forest service sign just before a gate. Go right and up at the sign bypassing private property to a sign pointing to Strapp Lakes. Continue straight on rocky tread up to a second sign and a three-way trail junction. Go left on the main trail and up to a junction at a bridge. You are now at the halfway point of the hike, and this is a good spot to turn around if you are not up to going the whole distance.

Going left takes you to the Red Rock Trailhead and Brainard Lake Road. Continue straight at the trail junction up to another three-way junction. The right fork is the Sourdough Trail and leads to Beaver Reservoir. Take the left fork, which will eventually pass by two junctions with the Waldrop Ski Trail. Avoid these trails and stay on the well-marked South St. Vrain Trail through beautiful spruce forests and small open meadows. Arrive at another trail junction on the left. This leads to Brainard Lake. Continue on the main trail on wooden planks through an often wet area. Cross over a small stream and climb out of the forest into an open meadow with spectacular views to the Indian Peaks. After a short distance the trail arrives at Brainard Lake Road, just below the Mitchell Creek Trailhead parking area.

Camping: Pawnee Campground, along the trail, and Brainard Lake Recreation Area.

12 Beaver Creek Trail

Highlights: This is a great hike that starts at the Beaver Creek Trailhead just west of Brainard Lake. Wildflowers, beautiful open tundra, and spectacular views to the plains and Mount Audubon are the main attractions of this hike. You can easily make this a two- to three-day hike and explore the trails near the Coney Flats Trailhead.

Season: April to late October.

Distance: 5.1 miles one-way.

Difficulty: Moderate to strenuous.

Map: Trails Illustrated Indian Peaks/Gold Hill, #102.

Management: Boulder Ranger District, USDA Forest Service.

Trail conditions: The lower section of the trail is well traveled, and the middle section is quite rocky as it cuts through open tundra on the way down to the Coney Flats Trailhead.

Finding the trailhead: From the junction of Broadway and Canyon in Boulder, go west on SR 119 for 16 miles to Nederland. Go west on SR 72 for 10 miles to Brainard Lake Road. Turn left on Brainard Lake Road past the Brainard Lake Recreation Site ($5.00 fee) to the Beaver Creek Trailhead.

Key points:

0.4   The trail cuts right up a steep switchback.

1.7   Junction with the Mount Audubon Trail.

4.8   Trailhead at Coney Flats.

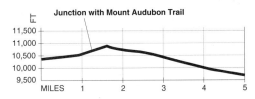

The hike: From the upper parking area, follow the well-marked Beaver Creek Trail. The trail makes a gradual climb up to a shelf and a junction with the Mount Audubon Trail. Wildflowers grow profusely along the trail and hillsides during the summer months. The trail is very wide and cuts up through a spruce forest to the trail junction with the Mount Audubon Trail. The Beaver Creek Trail goes right and down across beautiful open tundra. The high point of the hike is at the trail junction with the Mount Audubon Trail, and most of the hiking is downhill from that point on. The views to the open plains to the east and Mount Audubon and Mount Toll to the west are just splendid.

The trail cuts through the tundra to a saddle. After the saddle the trail drops down into a dense spruce forest and crosses branches of Beaver Creek to a series of steep switchbacks through a rocky area to the Coney Flats Trailhead. You can set up base camp near the Coney Flats Trailhead and explore the many trails in this section of the wilderness area.

Camping: Brainard Lake Recreation Area, along the trail, and at Coney Flats.

Beaver Creek Trail ● Mount Audubon Trail
Mitchell Lake Trail/Blue Lake Trail

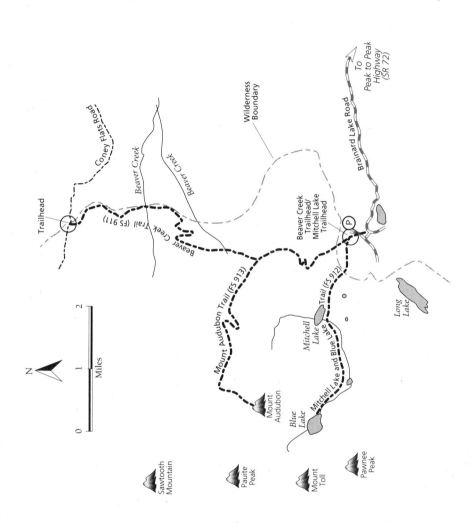

13 Mount Audubon Trail

See Map on Page 51

Highlights: This wonderful day hike ascends the beautiful alpine summit of Mount Audubon (13,223 feet). Wildflowers, panoramic alpine views, and alpine lakes make this hike well worth the effort. This is a very strenuous hike with a lot of altitude gain in a long 4-mile march to the summit. On the way to the summit there are stunning views out to Pawnee Peak, Mount Toll, Paiute Peak, Sawtooth Mountain, and Rocky Mountain National Park to the north. This is a very popular trail that sees a fair amount of traffic in the summer months. Your best bet to avoid the crowds would be to do the hike midweek.

Season: June to October.

Distance: 8 miles round-trip.

Difficulty: Strenuous.

Map: Trails Illustrated Indian Peaks/Gold Hill, #102.

Management: Boulder Ranger District, USDA Forest Service.

Trail conditions: The lower section of the trail is well traveled and has very loose, rocky tread to the summit.

Finding the trailhead: From the junction of SR 93 and SR 119 in Boulder, go west on SR 119 for 16 miles to Nederland. Go west on SR 72 for 10 miles to Brainard Lake Road. Turn left on Brainard Lake Road past the Brainard Lake Recreation Site ($5.00 fee) to the Mitchell Lake Trailhead parking area.

Key points:

0.4 The trail cuts right up a steep switchback.

1.3 Junction with the Beaver Creek Trail.

1.9 Great views out to the surrounding peaks and Blue Lake.

2.5 Steep switchbacks.

3.5 Steep switchbacks up to summit.

4.0 Mount Audubon summit.

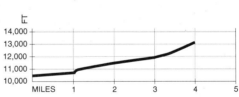

The hike: The hike starts at the Beaver Creek Trailhead, located at the Mitchell Lake Trailhead parking area above Brainard Lake. Access the well-marked Beaver Creek Trail on the north side of the parking area. The trail is well maintained and makes a gradual climb up to a shelf and the Mount Audubon Trail. After 0.5 mile of gentle terrain through a dense spruce forest, the trail makes a sharp right turn up a steep switchback with views out to the east. At 1.3 miles the Beaver Creek Trail goes right down to Coney Flats Road. Continue straight.

The trail now takes a tight line up through a stand of twisted krummholz pines and a small boulder field. You are gaining considerable altitude at this

Near the summit of Mount Audubon.

point, and the pine trees disappear behind you. The trail cuts over a small, beautiful stream and up through a stunning alpine meadow to a snowfield. At 2.5 miles the trail makes a sharp right away from the snowfield and climbs steeply through a boulder field to a broad, flat ridge with excellent views out to the surrounding alpine peaks.

At the 3.5-mile mark the trail goes left up a steep, rocky trail to the summit. There are a number of trails that shoot off from the main trail and take a steep scramble to the summit. Follow the cairns and stay on the main trail. It is easier to gain the summit by following the main trail, and it is less intrusive to the surrounding alpine environment.

After 4 miles you arrive at the summit of Mount Audubon (13,223 feet). The last section of the hike is above timberline and exposed to violent lightning storms. Get an early start and try and be off the summit by noon during the storm season of July and August. The last mile of the trail gains a thousand feet and can be very strenuous for those not acclimated to altitude. Take a break at one of the many rock shelters on the summit and enjoy the beautiful alpine scenery. C. C. Parry, a botanist, and zoologist J. W. Velie climbed the mountain in 1864 and named the peak after the famous naturalist, who never stepped foot in Colorado.

Camping: Brainard Lake Recreation Area.

14 Mitchell Lake Trail/ Blue Lake Trail

See Map on Page 51

Highlights: This day hike features breathtaking views to Paiute Peak, Mount Audubon, Little Pawnee Peak, and Pawnee Peak. In the summer months wildflowers are abundant, and Mitchell and Blue Lakes are two of the prettiest in the wilderness area.

Season: June to October.

Distance: 2.5 miles one-way.

Difficulty: Moderate.

Map: Trails Illustrated Indian Peaks/Gold Hill, #102.

Management: Boulder Ranger District, USDA Forest Service.

Trail conditions: The trail is well traveled and rocky on its lower section, with loose, rocky, and wet conditions up to Blue Lake. Expect to find snow on the upper section of the trail well into June.

Finding the trailhead: From the junction of Broadway and Canyon in Boulder, go west on SR 119 for 16 miles to Nederland. Go west on SR 72 for 10 miles to Brainard Lake Road. Go left on Brainard Lake Road past the Brainard Lake Recreation Site ($5.00 fee) and the Mitchell Lake Trailhead.

Key points:

0.2	Wilderness boundary.
0.8	Mitchell Lake.
1.0	Cross over Mitchell Creek.
1.5	Alpine meadow and ponds.
2.5	Blue Lake.

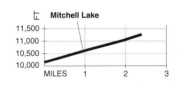

The hike: This is one of my favorite hikes in the Indian Peaks Wilderness Area, and judging by the number of people you will see on the trail in the summer months, it seems that many feel the same. If you are planning to hike up to Blue Lake during a summer weekend, arrive early to secure a parking space. The parking lot fills up quickly, and finding a space after 10:00 A.M. can be difficult.

The hike begins at the Mitchell Lake Trailhead, located near the bathrooms at the Mitchell Lake Trailhead parking area. The Mitchell Lake Trail begins at an elevation of 10,472 feet and climbs to 11,352 feet to Blue Lake in a little less than 2.5 miles. The start of the trail is wide, level, and somewhat rocky. At the 0.2-mile mark you enter the boundary of the wilderness area as the trail wanders through a dense spruce forest. At around the 0.3-mile mark you cross over Mitchell Creek on a wooden footbridge. After the footbridge the trail climbs gently up to Mitchell Lake, wildflowers, and spectacular views to Mount Audubon, Little Pawnee Peak, Mount Toll, and Paiute Peak. Mitchell Lake is a shallow, fourteen-acre lake that is stocked with cutthroat trout and is quite popular with anglers. The meadow around the lake is filled with wildflowers that grow profusely in the moist, fertile soil. Blanket flower, alpine primrose, mountain lupine, alpine aver, golden banner, and globe-flower are just a few of flowers that blossom around Mitchell Creek and Mitchell Lake.

At the 1-mile mark the trail crosses over Mitchell Creek on a makeshift bridge of logs and fallen trees. After Mitchell Creek the trail climbs on log steps up to a meadow with good views out to the surrounding peaks. This is another good place to stop and enjoy the views and the wildflowers. Wooden walkways guide you through the more marshy areas of the meadow and up to the drier, rocky section of the trail.

At around the 2-mile mark the trail cuts across a snowfield and follows rock cairns, with Mitchell Creek and Little Pawnee Peak on the left. At the 2.5-mile mark Blue Lake appears, situated in a cirque below the towering summits of Mount Toll and Paiute Peak. Blue Lake covers almost twenty-three acres, is almost a 100 feet deep, and is stocked with cutthroat trout. Take a lunch break and enjoy the panoramic views and alpine splendor.

Camping: Brainard Lake Recreation Area.

15 Lake Isabelle

Highlights: Mostly level trails, great views, and stunning wildflowers make this a perfect hike for the whole family. Take along a fishing rod and enjoy the fishing and views at Lake Isabelle.

Season: June to October.

Distance: 2 miles one-way.

Difficulty: Easy.

Map: Trails Illustrated Indian Peaks/Gold Hill, #102.

Management: Boulder Ranger District, USDA Forest Service.

Trail conditions: The trail up to the lake is well traveled and maintained.

Finding the trailhead: From the junction of SR 93 and SR 119 in Boulder, go west on SR 119 for 16 miles to Nederland. Go west on SR 72 for 10 miles to Brainard Lake Road. Go left on Brainard Lake Road past the Brainard Lake Recreation Site ($5.00 fee) to the Long Lake Trailhead.

Key points:

1.0   Pass Long Lake on the left.
2.0   Junction with Lake Isabelle Trail and Lake Isabelle.

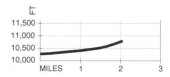

The hike: From the Long Lake Trailhead the trail remains fairly level as you hike along the

Lake Isabelle · Jean Luning Trail

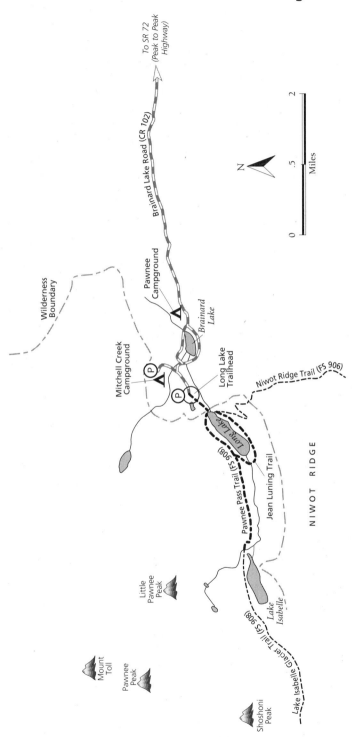

To SR 72
(Peak to Peak
Highway)

Brainard Lake Road (CR 102)

N

.5

Miles

0   2

Pawnee
Campground

Brainard
Lake

Wilderness
Boundary

Mitchell Creek
Campground

Long Lake
Trailhead

P

P

Niwot Ridge Trail (FS 906)

Long Lake

Pawnee Pass Trail (FS 908)

Jean Luning Trail

N I W O T   R I D G E

Little
Pawnee
Peak

Mount
Toll

Pawnee
Peak

Lake
Isabelle

Lake Isabelle Glacier Trail (FS 908)

Shoshoni
Peak

On the way to Lake Isabelle.

north side of Long Lake. At forty-and-a-half acres, Long Lake is the largest lake in the Indian Peaks Wilderness Area and is popular with anglers and hikers alike. Past Long Lake the trail becomes somewhat rocky and rooted and can be quite crowded with hikers during the late summer months. After 2 miles of mostly level hiking you come to Lake Isabelle. The lake is stocked with rainbow and cutthroat trout and can be fished with lures and artificial flies only. The views from the lake are quite spectacular, and wildflowers line the shore of the lake during the late summer months. Fred Fair from Boulder "discovered" the lake and glacier and named Isabelle Glacier and Lake Isabelle after his wife.

Options: For added mileage and excitement, follow the Isabelle Glacier Trail along the north side of Lake Isabelle for 1.7 miles to Isabelle Glacier. The trail is fairly level for the first 0.5 mile, then begins a steep climb up to a glacial pool just below Isabelle Glacier. Wildflowers, waterfalls, views, and glacial pools are the main attractions of this trail.

Camping: Brainard Lake Recreation Area and Pawnee Campground.

16 Jean Luning Trail

See Map on Page 56

Highlights: This great day hike makes a loop around Long Lake from the Long Lake Trailhead. Fishing, wildflowers, views, and easy hiking are the main attractions of this hike. Bring the family and a picnic lunch and enjoy one of the finest easy hikes in the wilderness area.

Season: June to October.

Distance: 2.7-mile loop.

Difficulty: Easy.

Map: Trails Illustrated Indian Peaks/Gold Hill, #102.

Management: Boulder Ranger District, USDA Forest Service.

Trail conditions: This popular trail is extremely smooth and well traveled.

Finding the trailhead: From the junction of SR 93 and SR 119 in Boulder, go west on SR 119 for 16 miles to Nederland. Go west on SR 72 for 10 miles to Brainard Lake Road. Go left on Brainard Lake Road past the Brainard Lake Recreation Site ($5.00 fee) to the Long Lake Trailhead.

Key points:

0.2 Go left on the Jean Luning Trail.

1.5 Go right on the Pawnee Pass Trail.

2.7 Back at the trailhead.

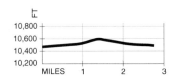

The hike: From the Long Lake Trailhead, travel 0.2 mile to the Jean Luning Trail. Go left on the Jean Luning near the eastern edge of Long Lake. The trail stays close to the southern shore of Long Lake and crosses through several marshy areas on wooden footbridges to the western end of the lake. Wildflowers are abundant near the shoreline and are quite striking during the summer months. The view west to Navajo, Apache, and Shoshoni Peaks are quite impressive and dominate the western skyline.

The trail is easy to follow and has minimal elevation gain up to the junction with the Pawnee Pass Trail at the western end of the lake, where the fishing is quite good. The lake is stocked with cutthroat, brook, and rainbow trout. Kids love this section of the trail and can easily entertain themselves along the lakeshore. Go right on the Pawnee Pass Trail for a little more than a mile of easy hiking to the parking area.

Camping: Brainard Lake Recreation Area and Pawnee Campground.

17 Pawnee Pass Trail

Highlights:	Located almost dead center in the Indian Peaks Wilderness Area, the Pawnee Pass Trail is a major trail running east to west, up to and over Pawnee Pass to the western side of the Indian Peaks Wilderness. Alpine vistas, alpine lakes, beautiful tundra, and wildflowers are the main attractions on this hike.
Season:	June to October.
Distance:	4.5 miles one-way.
Difficulty:	Strenuous.
Map:	Trails Illustrated Indian Peaks/Gold Hill, #102.
Management:	Boulder Ranger District, USDA Forest Service.
Trail conditions:	The lower section of the trail is well traveled; very loose, rocky tread to the summit.

Finding the trailhead: From the junction of SR 93 and SR 119 in Boulder, go west on SR 119 for 16 miles to Nederland. Go west on SR 72 for 10 miles to Brainard Lake Road. Go left on Brainard Lake Road past the Brainard Lake Recreation Site ($5.00 fee) to the Long Lake Trailhead.

Key points:

1.0 Pass Long Lake on the left.

2.0 Junction with Lake Isabelle Trail and Lake Isabelle.

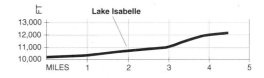

2.5 Steep switchbacks.

3.5 Saddle between Pawnee and Shoshoni Peaks.

4.1 Steep switchbacks up to Pawnee Pass.

4.5 Pawnee Pass.

Pawnee Pass Trail

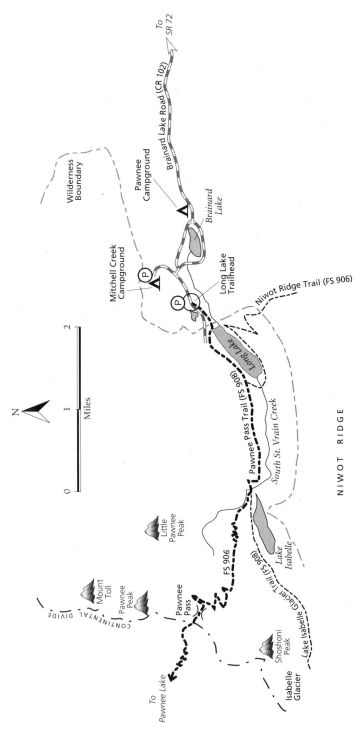

The hike: The trail gains more than 2,000 feet in 4.5 miles and offers some of the most beautiful scenery in the wilderness area. The trail is quite popular during the late summer months and sees heavy foot traffic. All along the length of the trail you are treated to beautiful mountain wildflowers, cascading waterfalls, jagged alpine peaks, and clear mountain lakes. This trail is a must-do hike in the Indian Peaks Wilderness Area.

From the Long Lake Trailhead, the trail remains fairly level as you hike along the north side of Long Lake. The trail is somewhat rocky and rooted and can be quite crowded with hikers during the late summer months. At forty-and-a-half acres, Long Lake is the largest lake in the Indian Peaks Wilderness Area and is popular with anglers and hikers alike. The lake is stocked with rainbow and cutthroat trout and can be fished with lures and artificial flies only. Views out to Apache, Navaho, and Shoshoni Peaks lure hikers ever upward.

At the 2-mile mark you come to a junction with Lake Isabelle and the Lake Isabelle Glacier Trail. Lake Isabelle sits in a commanding position below the jagged alpine summits of the aforementioned peaks. Glacial waters feed the lake, and wildflowers grow profusely along the lakeshore. The Pawnee Pass Trail goes right, away from the lake, and begins a steady climb up to a ridge high above the lake. The trail in this section climbs steeply on rocky switchbacks and offers incredible views down to Lake Isabelle and upward to the surrounding peaks. After the steep switchbacks, the trail surprisingly levels out on a saddle between Shoshoni Peak to the south and Pawnee Peak to the north. This is a great place to rest and take in the views before the final grunt to the top of Pawnee Pass.

At the 4.1-mile mark the trail traverses on several long, steep switchbacks up to the top of Pawnee Pass. Pawnee Pass is very exposed to the elements

High above Lake Isabelle on the Pawnee Pass Trail.

ot the greatest place to hang out during high winds or stormy weather. ware of oncoming storms before spending any time on the pass. If you the time and energy and the weather is not threatening, go west to take in the views down to Pawnee Lake.

Camping: Brainard Lake Recreation Area and at Pawnee Lake, on the western side of Pawnee Pass.

---

18 Niwot Ridge Trail

Highlights:	This hike travels up to and across Niwot Ridge. Beautiful vistas, wildflowers, and alpine tundra are the main attractions of this wonderful day hike.
Season:	June to October.
Distance:	2.7 miles one-way.
Difficulty:	Moderate.
Map:	Trails Illustrated Indian Peaks/Gold Hill, #102.
Management:	Boulder Ranger District, USDA Forest Service.
Trail conditions:	The lower portion of the trail is well maintained; rocky and steep across the tundra.

Finding the trailhead: From the junction of SR 93 and SR 119 in Boulder, go west on SR 119 for 16 miles to Nederland. Go west on SR 72 for 10 miles to Brainard Lake Road. Go left on Brainard Lake Road past the Brainard Lake Recreation Site ($5.00 fee) to the Long Lake Trailhead.

Key points:

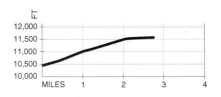

- 0.2 Go left on the Jean Luning Trail.
- 0.4 Go left on the faint Niwot Ridge Trail.
- 1.8 Sign for Niwot Ridge Alpine Research Area.
- 2.7 Research hut.

The hike: The Niwot Ridge Trail sees very little traffic and takes you up to and on Niwot Ridge, a beautiful stretch of alpine tundra located above the Isabelle Lake drainage. The views in all directions from the ridge are breathtaking. The views north to Rocky Mountain National Park are exceptional, so bring a camera.

The hike starts at the Long Lake Trailhead and travels a short distance on the Pawnee Pass Trail. At an obvious trail junction go left on the Jean Luning Trail on the south side of Long Lake. Follow the trail across several wooden footbridges, looking for a trail on the left. The Niwot Ridge Trail is not marked, so look hard for a trail that heads left into the tall spruce trees. Go left on the Niwot Ridge Trail into the wood and begin climbing up and to the east. The trail climbs up through a wet area filled with beautiful yellow snow buttercups.

Niwot Ridge Trail

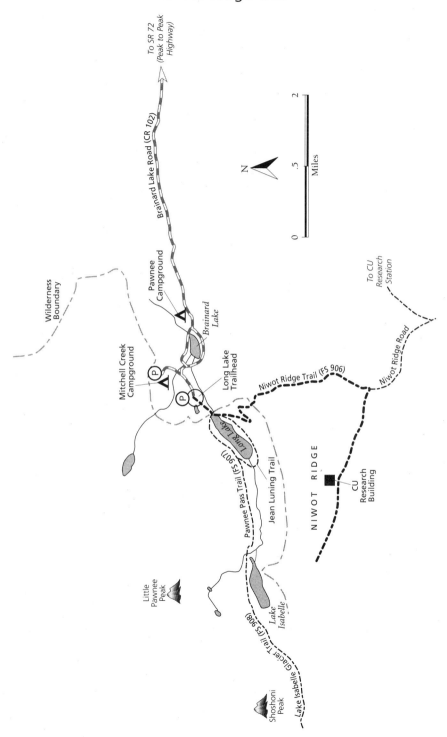

To SR 72
(Peak to Peak Highway)

Brainard Lake Road (CR 102)

N

0   .5   2
Miles

To CU Research Station

Wilderness Boundary

Pawnee Campground

Brainard Lake

Mitchell Creek Campground

P

Long Lake Trailhead

P

Niwot Ridge Trail (FS 906)

Niwot Ridge Road

Long Lake

Pawnee Pass Trail (FS 907)

Jean Luning Trail

N I W O T   R I D G E

CU Research Building

Little Pawnee Peak

Lake Isabelle

Glacier Trail (FS 908)

Shoshoni Peak

Lake Isabelle

After a mile of steep hiking the trail gains Niwot Ridge and tundra. The trail is quite narrow and rocky, and the views up the Isabelle Lake drainage are gorgeous. Follow the narrow, rocky trail to a sign for the Niwot Ridge Alpine Research Area. The area is one of only seventeen long-term ecological research stations established by the National Science Foundation in the United States. Please respect the work that the foundation has done on Niwot Ridge and tread lightly through this delicate, ecological wonder.

The trail now traverses across the tundra, heading south through an area of krummholz pines, low-lying, wind-blown trees that live in harsh alpine conditions. Some of the trees in this area are estimated to be at least 2,000 years old. After a mile of level hiking through the tundra, the trail goes west toward an obvious road leading up Niwot Ridge toward Arikaree Peak (13,150 feet). Follow the road up along a fenceline to a hut on the right. The hut is used for lightning research, and people can be seen scurrying around during the summer months. The views to Navajo Peak are wonderful, and this makes a great turnaround point.

Camping: Brainard Lake Recreation Area.

19 Sourdough Trail South

Highlights:	This great trail is along the eastern flank of Niwot Mountain. Dense pine forests, wildflowers, easy access to connecting trails, and views are the main attractions of this hike.
Season:	April to early November.
Distance:	6.2 miles one-way.
Difficulty:	Moderate to strenuous.
Map:	Trails Illustrated Indian Peaks/Gold Hill, #102.
Management:	Boulder Ranger District, USDA Forest Service.
Trail conditions:	This popular trail is smooth in some sections and extremely rocky in others.

Finding the trailhead: From the intersection of Canyon and Broadway in Boulder, go west on Canyon (SR 119) for 16 miles to Nederland. Go right on SR 72 (Peak to Peak Highway) for 6 miles to CR 116 (toward the University of Colorado Research Station) and go 0.5 mile to a large parking area on the left and the trailhead.

Key points:

0.3	Small bridge.
0.8	Power lines.
1.8	Trail junction.
2.7	Bridge.

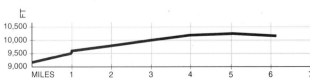

Sourdough Trail South

5.3   Junction with the Little Raven Ski Trail.
6.2   Brainard Lake Road.

The hike: The Sourdough Trail (FS 835) parallels the Peak to Peak Highway and stretches almost 18 miles from Rainbow Lakes Road at its southern end to Peaceful Valley in the north. Along the way the trail connects with several trails around the Brainard Lake Recreation Area and the Peaceful Valley Campground. With the help of a map and compass, you can connect with other trails for a variety of loops and distances from short day hikes to multiday excursions. The best way to hike the Sourdough Trail is by car shuttling from various trailheads. This eliminates any backtracking, and you can cover more territory this way.

This hike goes south to north, starting at Rainbow Lakes Road and traveling north to Brainard Lake Road. The trail is quite popular with mountain bikers and trailrunners during the summer months, so be on the lookout for other trail users. An excellent ski or snowshoe tour during the winter months, the trail should be free of snow by late April early May and remains green until late October or early November.

The trail stays mostly in the tall pines and is sheltered from the wind. From the parking area cross CR 116 and follow the obvious trail into the woods. The trail climbs at a gentle grade through a dense forest of lodge-pole and spruce evergreens. At the power lines there are views to the east. The trail becomes rocky as you drop down a short hill, then climbs up to a trail junction at the 1.8-mile mark. The trail now climbs up to a small ridge and again drops to a bridge crossing at the 2.7-mile mark. This is a good spot to take a break.

Past the bridge the trail follows a series of narrow switchbacks, gaining a fair amount of elevation. At the 4-mile mark the trail wanders through tall pines into a small open meadow with views to the east and north. You come to a junction with the Little Raven Ski Trail on the left at the 5.3-mile mark. Continue straight up a steep, rocky section to an often wet area and a bridge. Cross the bridge, then make a short jog up to Brainard Lake Road and your turn-around point.

Camping: Rainbow Lakes Campground, along the trail, and at Brainard Lake Recreation Area.

20 Rainbow Lakes

Highlights:	This easy hike traverses through a dense spruce forest up to ten well-stocked lakes and ponds located less than 1 mile from the trailhead. Pack a lunch and take along a fishing rod.
Season:	May to October.
Distance:	2 miles round-trip.
Difficulty:	Easy.
Map:	Trails Illustrated Indian Peaks/Gold Hill, #102.
Management:	Boulder Ranger District, USDA Forest Service.
Trail conditions:	The trail is maintained and sees heavy use on weekend days in the summer months.

Finding the trailhead: From the junction of SR 93 and SR 119 in Boulder, go west on SR 119 for 16 miles to Nederland. Go west on SR 72 (Peak to Peak Highway) for 6 miles to CR 116. Go left on CR 116 to the Rainbow Lakes Campground and the trailhead.

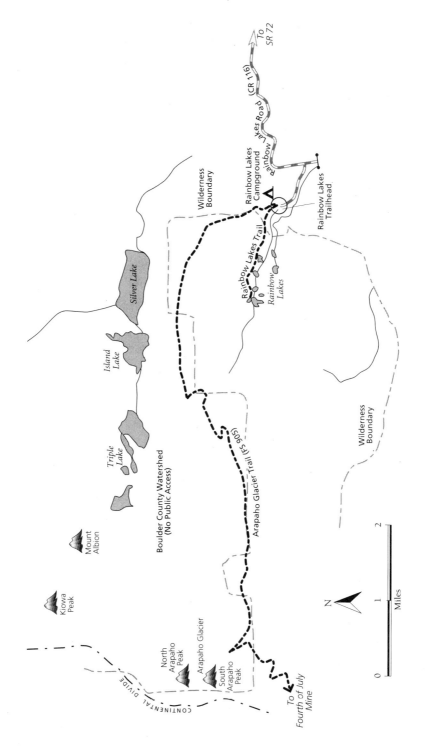

0.3   A faint trail goes off to the right to two unnamed lakes.

0.4   The first of the Rainbow Lakes.

0.9   The end of the trail, between two lakes.

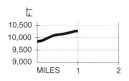

The hike: This is a short hike up to a cluster of ten lakes and ponds ranging in size from one to three acres. The popular trail has little elevation gain and sees a lot of foot traffic from anglers and hikers alike. Camping is allowed near the lake, but most parties camp at the Rainbow Lakes Campground near the trailhead and hike to the lakes from there. The lakes are quite charming and are surrounded by dense spruce forest, with thick grasses and willow bushes lining the shoreline. The lakes are stocked with cutthroat and rainbow trout.

Camping: Rest rooms and camping are available at Rainbow Lakes Campground, at the trailhead. Camping is also allowed near the lake.

21 Arapaho Glacier Trail

See Map on Page 67

Highlights: Abundant wildflowers, alpine lakes, and spectacular views of Arapaho Peak and Arapaho Glacier are the highlights of this long day hike, which has considerable elevation gain and loss. If you can arrange a shuttle, have one party park at Rainbow Lakes Campground and the other at Buckingham Campground at the Fourth of July Trailhead.

Season: June to October.

Distance: 6 miles one-way.

Difficulty: Strenuous.

Map: Trails Illustrated Indian Peaks/Gold Hill, #102.

Management: Boulder Ranger District, USDA Forest Service.

Trail conditions: The trail sees a lot of use and is well maintained.

Finding the trailhead: From the junction of SR 93 and SR 119 in Boulder, go west on SR 119 for 16 miles to Nederland. Go west on SR 72 (Peak to Peak Highway) for 6 miles to CR 116. Go left on CR 116 to the Rainbow Lakes Campground and the trailhead.

Key points:

0.4   Boulder County Watershed fence line. No access to the right.

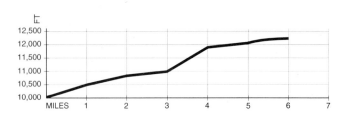

The hike: From the trailhead follow the well-marked Arapaho Glacier Trail up into the tall pine trees. You slowly gain altitude as the trail parallels a fence line along the Boulder County Watershed (closed to the public) property on the right. At 1 mile the trail becomes severely rutted, rocky, and rough as you follow it up to timberline. At 2 miles the trail passes through an area of beautiful twisted pine trees into the open tundra. Wildflowers cover the ground, and small snow-fed creeks trickle down along the trail, adding to the mountain experience. Above timberline the views become extremely striking. Off to the right are Silver, Albion, and Goose Lakes, which, when combined with the towering summits of Arikaree and Kiowa Peaks filling the skyline, make for a picturesque alpine setting. This is a great spot to take a break and enjoy the impressive alpine scenery. Don't be tempted to hike down to the lakes within the Boulder County Watershed, or you will be hit with a hundred dollar fine for trespassing and a blow to your ego.

At 2.8 miles the trail takes a sharp left away from the lakes, and the climbing begins in earnest. This is backcountry hiking at its finest: panoramic views, alpine flowers, high alpine peaks, and glacier-fed lakes. On the right the rugged summits of South and North Arapaho Peaks, at 13,502 feet, dominate the skyline. The grade of the trail eases as you traverse a ridgeline toward the Arapaho Glacier Overlook. At the 6-mile mark you arrive at the Arapaho Glacier Overlook, and if you're smart you will take a well-deserved break before heading back to the trailhead. Several rock shelters located near the overlook are protected from high winds and snow.

Looking west on the Arapaho Glacier Trail near the Goose Lake overlook.

The Arapaho Glacier has a storied and colorful history. Herbert Wheeler of the U.S. Forest Service, and his brother-in-law D. M. Andrews, a local botanist, discovered the glacier on a day trip looking for alpine wildflowers. The pair walked across the glacier, first noticing small cracks in the ice, then much larger ones several feet across. The glacier filled the cirque on the eastern side of the two Arapaho Peaks and was estimated to be a least 0.5-mile across. The discovery of the glacier was quite a boom for local tourism and was heavily promoted by the Boulder Chamber of Commerce. Fred Fair, a local businessman, secured permission from the Boulder County commissioners to build a road to the overlook just above the glacier. The road was to be built in stages, with the first section reaching what is now the Rainbow Lakes Campground. Underestimating the cost of the project, Mr. Fair teamed up with a Colorado Springs millionaire who was willing to invest the much-needed cash to complete the project. But there was a catch. Mr. Fair's wealthy investor wanted to turn the highway into a toll road and charge tourists for the ride up to the glacier. Instead, Mr. Fair operated a scaled-down version of the project that shuttled tourists into the area close to the glacier by automobile. They were then brought up the glacier via horseback, where they enjoyed a short stay on the ice, throwing snowballs and sliding down the glacier before heading back to Boulder.

The Denver & Interurban Railroad, as part of a promotion to get tourists up to the glacier, offered a thousand-dollar prize to the first aviator willing to land his airplane on the glacier. A young stunt flyer who went by the nickname "Slim" was more than willing to give it a go until Mr. Fair took one look at his feeble plane and reneged on the offer. Slim—better known today by his given name, Charles Lindbergh—later took his plane and flew across the big pond to Paris and fame.

The city of Boulder then purchased 3,869 acres just east of the Arapaho Peaks from the federal government for a mere $1.25 per acre, thus securing a clean water source, a glacier of its own, and dooming Mr. Fair's road to the glacier. Starting in 1939, the Boulder Chamber of Commerce led group hikes up to the glacier, starting at the Fourth of July Trailhead, and more than 200 people participated in the inaugural hike. Today, the group hikes no longer exist, and walking on Arapaho Glacier is a no-no, but don't let that stop you from making the long hike up to one of the most beautiful spots in the Indian Peaks Wilderness.

Camping: Rest rooms and camping are available at Rainbow Lakes Campground, at the trailhead.

22 Mineral Mountain

Highlights: This is a nice excursion up to Mineral Mountain with excellent views to the east and west. Beautiful wildflowers cover the hillsides. The view from Caribou Flats to the Indian Peaks is spectacular.

Season: June to October.

Distance: 5.6 miles one-way.

Difficulty: Moderate.

Map: Trails Illustrated Indian Peaks/Gold Hill, #102.

Management: Boulder Ranger District, USDA Forest Service.

Trail conditions: The hike follows an old jeep road and is very rocky in some sections.

Finding the trailhead: From the junction of SR 93 and SR 119 in Boulder, go west on SR 119 for 16 miles to Nederland. Go south on SR 119 for 0.5 mile to the Eldora turnoff. Turn right and go 3.2 miles on SR 130 to the town of Eldora. Park at the intersection of Eldorado Avenue and Sixth Street.

Key points:

0.1   Go right.

1.2   Small pond on the right.

2.7   Steep hill.

3.4   Trail junction.

3.7   Flat area.

4.5   Road junction.

4.7   Three-way junction.

5.6   Caribou Townsite.

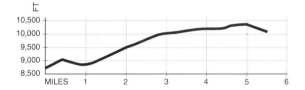

The hike: From downtown Eldora head up Washington Avenue toward a cabin with elk horns on the front. Go right at the cabin up a rocky, rough jeep road. There are great views to the east as the trail veers away from Eldora and winds along the base of Eldorado Mountain up through an aspen forest to a small pond at the 1.2-mile mark. The hillsides around the pond are covered with beautiful alpine flowers during the summer months and look like a scene out of *The Sound of Music*.

At around the 1.7-mile mark the trail becomes steep and rocky as it climbs along the north flank of Mineral Mountain. For almost 2 miles the trail climbs up to a trail junction with an old mining road on the left. Go right at the trail junction up a short, steep rocky hill up to a level area at the 3.7-mile mark. Here the trail becomes flat and cuts across open meadows covered with bristlecone pines and beautiful alpine flowers. There are spectacular views here to the north and west. Great camping exists along the trail for the next mile.

Mineral Mountain

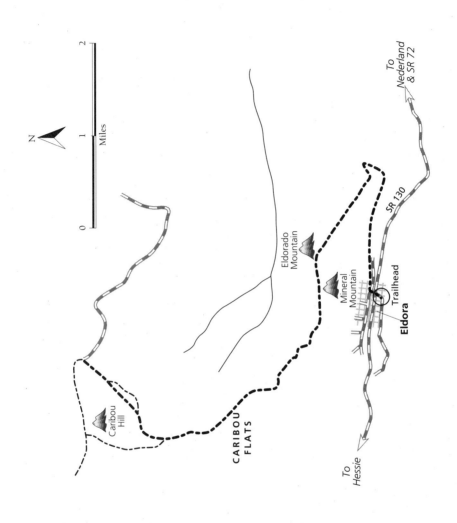

At the 4.5-mile mark you arrive at a road junction; continue straight up to a three-way split in the road. At the split go right and down into what was the old Caribou Townsite. Silver was discovered at Caribou in 1869, and by 1870 more than thirty mines were in operation. The town thrived for more than ten years, and it is estimated that more than twenty million dollars in silver was taken from the mines during that time. Houses, saloons, and hotels were constructed to support the ever-growing population. The town and its people prospered until a number of tragedies struck. Scarlet fever and diphtheria almost wiped out the younger population, and after the fire of 1879 the town never recovered. A few of the original foundations are all that remain of what was a thriving mining town. From Caribou retrace your route back to Eldora.

Camping: Along the trail.

23 Arapaho Pass Trail to Lake Dorothy

Highlights:	This is a fantastic day hike up to Lake Dorothy via the Arapaho Pass Trail, one of the best trails in the wilderness area for viewing wildflowers.
Season:	June to October.
Distance:	3.2 miles one-way.
Difficulty:	Moderate to strenuous.
Map:	Trails Illustrated Indian Peaks/Gold Hill, #102.
Management:	Boulder Ranger District, USDA Forest Service.
Trail conditions:	The lower section of the Arapaho Pass Trail is extremely popular during the summer months and sees heavy traffic on the weekends. The lower section of the trail stays wet early in the season; the upper section is rocky up to Arapaho Pass.

Finding the trailhead: From the junction of SR 93 and SR 119 in Boulder, go west on SR 119 for 16 miles to Nederland. Go south on SR 119 for 0.5 mile to the Eldora turnoff. Go right on SR 130 into the town of Eldora. As the road turns into CR 111, continue straight for 5.2 miles to the Buckingham Campground and the trailhead.

Key points:

0.0   Arapaho Pass Trailhead.
1.0   Junction with the Diamond Lake Trail.
1.7   Junction with the Arapaho Glacier Trail.
2.7   Arapaho Pass.
3.2   Lake Dorothy.

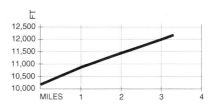

Arapaho Pass Trail to Lake Dorothy • Diamond Lake

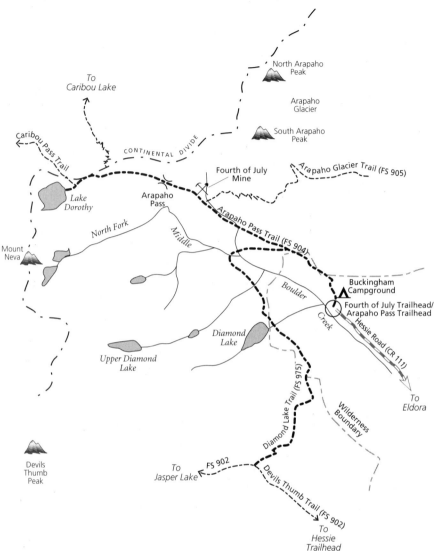

The hike: Begin at the Arapaho Pass Trailhead. Follow the well-marked trail and begin climbing up to the Diamond Lake Trailhead. The start of the trail passes through a dense forest on wooden planks up through an often wet area. Be on the lookout for purple fringe, golden banner, rosy paintbrush, and other water-loving wildflowers for the next mile. The trail climbs steeply and crosses over several glacier-fed streams coming down the steep slopes to the north. The steep forested slopes are saturated with a variety of wildflowers that are a feast for the eyes, and the views to the summits of Devils Thumb, Mount Neva, and Satanta Peak to the south and west are beautiful.

After a mile of steep hiking you arrive at a junction with the Diamond Lake Trail (see Hike 24). The Arapaho Pass Trail goes to the right and up through an often wet area on a steep hillside filled with wildflowers during the summer months. Continue climbing on good tread, and at 1.5 miles you gain a shelf just below the Fourth of July Mine. The shelf has several small streams flowing through it and stays wet even in the driest years. At the 1.7-mile mark you arrive at a trail junction and the Fourth of July Mine. The Arapaho Glacier Trail (see Hike 21) goes up and right. Be on the lookout for elephant heads that grow around the stream and moist areas near the mine. This small pinkish-purple flower looks like a small elephant's head, complete with ears and a long curved trunk. Continue straight up the obvious Arapaho Pass Trail and begin a long climb on rocky tread up to Arapaho Pass. Upper Diamond Lake and several unnamed lakes can be seen to the south and west. The views west to Devils Thumb and Mount Neva are sensational, and the twin summits of South and North Arapaho Peaks can be seen to the northeast in the distant skyline. Before you know it, you arrive at Arapaho Pass (11,906 feet) and a trail junction.

The Arapaho Pass Trail drops steeply down and switchbacks to the right to Caribou Lake and Coyote Park. To reach Lake Dorothy, continue straight (west) up on the Caribou Pass Trail. After a short 0.5-mile of hiking, go left to the lake across rocky talus and enjoy a well-deserved rest and a snack. Lake Dorothy is the highest lake (12,061 feet) in the Indian Peaks Wilderness and is a great spot for fishing and just hanging out. The lake is situated on a rocky shelf below Mount Neva with impressive, towering rock walls on its western side.

Camping: Buckingham Campground.

Beautiful Lake Dorothy with Mount Neva in the background.

24 Diamond Lake

See Map on Page 74

Highlights: This is a great short day hike up to a beautiful alpine lake surrounded by towering, rocky summits. The views on the first section of the trail are spectacular. Expect to see wildflowers, cascading glacier-fed waterfalls, and great views out to Woodland Mountain, Devils Thumb, and Mount Neva.

Season: June to October.

Distance: 2.5 miles one-way.

Difficulty: Moderate.

Map: Trails Illustrated Indian Peaks/Gold Hill, #102.

Management: Boulder Ranger District, USDA Forest Service.

Trail conditions: The lower section of the trail is very popular and stays wet well into the summer months. The section from the Arapaho Pass Trail up to the lake is extremely wet, and there are several stream crossings. Expect to get wet. Most sections of the trail are well marked and easy to follow.

Finding the trailhead: From the junction of SR 93 and SR 119 in Boulder, go west on SR 119 for 16 miles to Nederland. Go south on SR 119 for 0.5 mile to the Eldora turnoff. Go right on SR 130 into the town of Eldora. As the road turns into CR 111, continue straight for 5.2 miles to the Buckingham Campground and the trailhead.

Key points:

0.0 Arapaho Pass Trailhead (FS 904).

1.0 Junction with the Diamond Lake Trail (FS 975).

1.3 Cross over Boulder Creek.

2.5 Arrive at Diamond Lake.

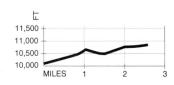

The hike: Diamond Lake is a fourteen-acre stream-fed alpine lake situated in a valley below Arapaho Pass. The lake is stocked with brook, rainbow, and cutthroat trout and is a popular destination for day-hikers, backpackers, and anglers. The trail sees heavy traffic and is quite busy during the weekends in the summer months. Snow stays on the upper section of the trail well into late June or early July. Don't venture off the trail, doing so only creates useless spur trails and erosion. This is a great hike for families.

Begin at the Arapaho Pass Trailhead. Follow the well-marked trail and begin to climb up to the Diamond Lake Trailhead. The start of the trail passes through a dense forest on wooden planks up through an often wet area. Be on the lookout for purple fringe, golden banner, rosy paintbrush, and other water-loving wildflowers for the next mile. The trail climbs steeply and crosses over several glacier-fed streams coming down the steep slopes to the north.

The views to the summits of Devils Thumb and Mount Neva to the w
are spectacular.

After a mile of steep hiking you arrive at the start of the Diamond Lake
Trail. Go left and drop down to the north fork of Middle Boulder Creek. The
next section of the trail is a wildflower bonanza: The flowers light up the
trail like Christmas lights and are strewn everywhere along the steep hillsides and wet areas. Golden banner, avalanche lily, western wallflowers, black-
eyed Susan, mountain dryad, and whiplash daisy are the most common flowers
found in the moist, rich soil along the trail.

At the 1.3-mile mark you cross over the north fork of Middle Boulder Creek
on a wooden bridge. The trail is rocky, wet, and rutted through this section.
Stay on the main trail and expect to get wet. Snow stays on the trail well
into late June or early July, and following the trail can be difficult. Be on the
lookout for trail markers.

After crossing several wet sections you start to climb up to a bench and
a beautiful alpine meadow. Wooden planks carry you over the wet section
of the meadow and to a trail marker and the lake on the right. The views
from the lake are incredible and explain why the trail is so popular. Take a
break and enjoy the scenery and beauty of the surrounding mountains.

Options: Spend the night at the lake, catch some fish, or just relax. Follow
the Diamond Lake Trail (FS 975) south to the Devils Thumb Trail (FS 902).
Go west to Jasper Lake or east back to the Hessie Trailhead for a wonderful two- to three-day trip.

Camping: Buckingham Campground or along the shoreline of Diamond Lake
(by permit only; see Appendix A for permit-issuing locations).

Early summer at Diamond Lake.

Highlights: This is a short, sweet hike up to small, lovely Lost Lake, located just outside the boundary of the Indian Peaks Wilderness Area and 1.5 miles from the old town site of Hessie. Fishing, wildflowers, waterfalls, and a beautiful mountain stream are just a few of the highlights of this hike. This is a great snowshoe or backcountry ski tour in the winter months. However, note that the road is closed during the winter beyond the west end of Eldora, adding an extra 3.5 miles to the total distance.

Season: May to November.

Distance: 3.4 miles round-trip.

Difficulty: Easy.

Map: Trails Illustrated Indian Peaks/Gold Hill, #102.

Management: Boulder Ranger District, USDA Forest Service.

Trail conditions: The trail up to Lost Lake is very popular and well maintained.

Finding the trailhead: From the junction of SR 93 and SR 119 in Boulder, go west on SR 119 for 16 miles to Nederland. Go south on SR 119 for 0.5 mile to the Eldora turnoff. Go right for 3.2 miles to the town of Eldora. Continue straight for 1.5 miles to a road junction. Go left past the old town site of Hessie to the trailhead. The last 0.8 mile of road may not be suitable for low-clearance or two-wheel-drive vehicles.

Key points:

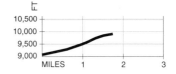

0.0 Hessie Trailhead.

0.9 Junction with the Devils Thumb and Devils Thumb Bypass Trails. Go straight over the bridge, following the Devils Thumb Trail.

1.3 Lost Lake Trail.

1.7 Arrive at Lost Lake.

3.4 Back at Hessie Trailhead.

The hike: From the trailhead follow the wide four-wheel-drive road up to the Devils Thumb Bypass Trail. This section of the trail climbs gently along the south fork of Middle Boulder Creek on a rocky, wide old road. In the summer expect to see many wildflowers as the hills along the trail are covered with mountain dryad, nelson larkspur, creeping hollygrape, and yellow stonecrop.

After 0.5 mile the trail becomes very rocky and parallels Boulder Creek. There are some rocks on the left that are a great place to stop, relax, and enjoy the rushing waters of Boulder Creek. The runoff waters of late spring and early summer are quite impressive as they flow down from the high peaks. After a little less than a mile of hiking you come to a junction with

Lost Lake

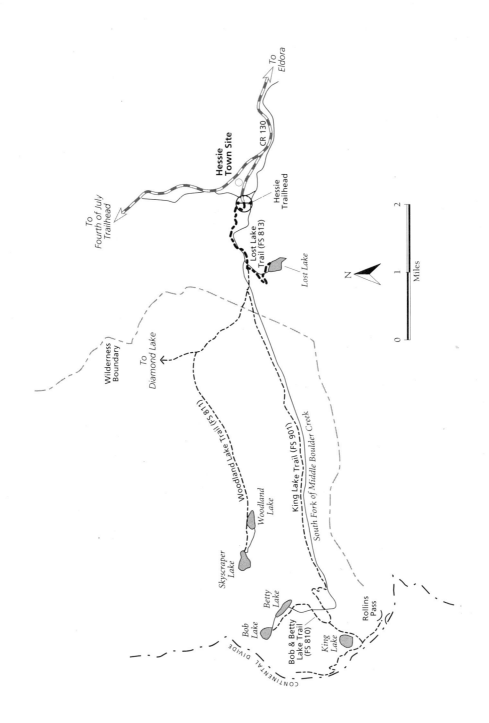

Thumb Bypass Trail on the right. Cross the bridge over Middle ~~eek~~ and climb a short distance up to the Lost Lake Trail, on the on the Lost Lake Trail traveling through a dense spruce forest ~~o~~ gently up to Lost Lake. The narrow trail winds up and into trees, ~~cr~~ossing a small footbridge and then climbing steeply up to the lake.

Lost Lake, which is stocked with rainbow and brook trout, is a great spot for fishing and picnicking. Take a break and enjoy a long lunch by the lake before heading back to the trailhead.

Eldora, once a rough-and-tumble mining town of the Old West, is now a small mountain town with a handful of year-round residents. In 1989 the Eldora Historic District was formed, and sixty-seven buildings were placed on the National Register of Historic Places. The town was originally called Happy Valley after a placer claim by John H. Kemp in 1891. Word spread of the occasional gold strike, and the town grew to a whopping 1,000 hearty miners, call girls, and saloon owners. Around 1898 the name of the town was changed to Camp Eldorado, but the U.S. Postal Service had a tough time getting the mail there, sending it instead to Eldorado, California. The name was then shortened to Eldora. By the early 1900s the boomtown went bust, and today Eldora is a quiet, scenic mountain town and the gateway to the southern Indian Peaks.

Camping: Near the trailhead and along the trail.

---

26 Devils Thumb Trail to Jasper Lake

Highlights:	This is a wonderful hike up to beautiful Jasper Lake. Jasper Lake is a nineteen-acre glacier and stream-fed alpine lake situated in a dense spruce forest below the jagged summit of Devils Thumb Peak and the curving ridgeline of Mount Neva. Expect to see abundant wildflowers, alpine lakes, and spectacular views of Devils Thumb Peak and Mount Neva. Snow stays on the trail above the Diamond Lake Trail well into late June. Cutthroat, brook, and brown trout can be found in the clear waters of the lake; bring a fishing rod along.
Season:	May to November.
Distance:	4.5 miles one-way.
Difficulty:	Moderate.
Map:	Trails Illustrated Indian Peaks/Gold Hill, #102.
Management:	Boulder Ranger District, USDA Forest Service.
Trail conditions:	The lower portion of the trail is maintained and sees heavy use during the late summer months. The upper portion of the trail is rocky, wet, and covered with snow during the late spring and early summer months.

Devils Thumb Trail to Jasper Lake

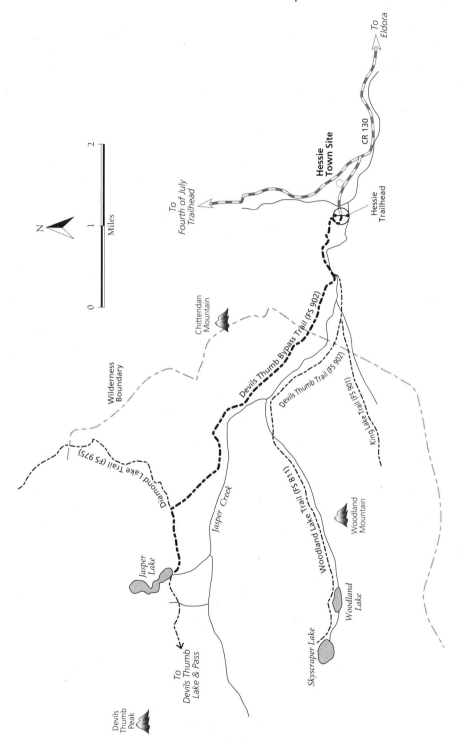

Finding the trailhead: From the junction of SR 93 and SR 119 in Boulder, go west on SR 119 for 16 miles to Nederland. Go south on SR 119 for 0.5 mile to the Eldora turnoff. Go right for 3.2 miles to the town of Eldora. Continue straight for 1.5 miles to a road junction. Go left pass the old town site of Hessie to the trailhead. The last 0.8 mile of road may not be suitable for low-clearance or two-wheel-drive vehicles.

Key points:

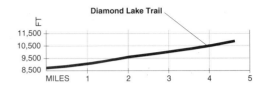

0.0	Hessie Trailhead.
1.0	Junction with the Devils Thumbs and Devils Thumb Bypass Trails. Go right up the Devils Thumb Bypass Trail.
1.7	Enter the Indian Peaks Wilderness Boundary.
2.1	Junction with the Devils Thumb Trail.
3.9	Junction with the Diamond Lake Trail.
4.5	Jasper Lake.

The hike: From the trailhead follow the wide four-wheel-drive road up to the Devils Thumb Bypass Trail. This section of the trail climbs gently along the south fork of Middle Boulder Creek on rocky tread. In the summer expect to see many wildflowers as the hills along the trail are covered with mountain dryad, nelson larkspur, creeping hollygrape, and yellow stonecrop.

After 0.5 mile the trail becomes very rocky and parallels Boulder Creek. There are some rocks on the left that make a great place to stop, relax, and

Crossing Jasper Creek.

enjoy the rushing waters of Boulder Creek. The runoff waters of late spring and early summer are quite impressive as they flow down from the high peaks.

At the 1-mile mark go right, just before a bridge, on the steep, Devils Thumb Bypass Trail. The trail climbs steeply away from Boulder Creek on rocky tread through a dense conifer forest. After a short distance the trail becomes narrow and level as you make your way through an open meadow to the boundary of the Indian Peaks Wilderness Area. Be on the lookout for moss campion, marsh marigold, and other water-loving wildflowers along this section of the trail.

Around 2.1 miles you come to a junction with the Devils Thumb Trail; go right. Here you begin a good climb on rocky tread up to the Diamond Lake Trail. Creeping dryads are particularly abundant along the trail, especially in the wet areas. The trail is often wet and follows a drainage for a short section. As you gain altitude the views open up to Woodland Mountain on the left, Devils Thumb Peak straight ahead, and Mount Neva and Arapaho Pass on the right.

After you pass the Diamond Lake Trail it is just a short hike up to Jasper Lake. Snow stays on the trail until mid-July, and the trail can be hard to follow in the late spring and early summer months. At 4.5 miles you arrive at beautiful Jasper Lake. Take a break and enjoy the views of the surrounding mountains and serene lake setting.

Camping: Rest rooms and camping are available at the trailhead.

27 Southern Loop

Highlights:	This is a spectacular two- or three-day hike that takes you deep into the southern part of the Indian Peaks Wilderness Area. This loop will take you to beautiful mountain streams, high alpine lakes, towering rocky peaks, and open flower-filled meadows. Wildflowers grow profusely during the summer months, and the scenery is spectacular.
Season:	Late June to early October.
Distance:	14.9-mile loop.
Difficulty:	Moderate to difficult.
Map:	Trails Illustrated Indian Peaks/Gold Hill, #102.
Management:	Boulder Ranger District, USDA Forest Service.
Trail conditions:	The lower part of the trail is maintained and well marked. The upper portions of the hike follow sections of steep, rocky tread.

Finding the trailhead: From the junction of SR 93 and SR 119 in Boulder, go west on SR 119 for 16 miles to Nederland. Go south on SR 119 for 0.5 mile to the Eldora turnoff. Go right for 3.2 miles to the town of Eldora. Continue straight for 1.5 miles to a road junction. Go left past the old town site

Southern Loop

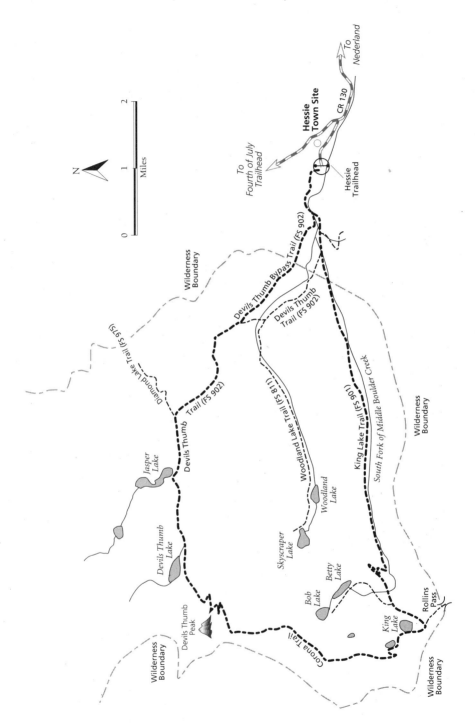

To Nederland

Hessie Town Site

CR 130

To Fourth of July Trailhead

Hessie Trailhead

Devils Thumb Bypass Trail (FS 902)

Wilderness Boundary

Devils Thumb Trail (FS 902)

Diamond Lake Trail (FS 975)

Woodland Lake Trail (FS 811)

King Lake Trail (FS 901)

South Fork of Middle Boulder Creek

Devils Thumb Trail (FS 902)

Jasper Lake

Devils Thumb Lake

Devils Thumb Peak

Wilderness Boundary

Corona Trail

Skyscraper Lake

Woodland Lake

Bob Lake

Betty Lake

King Lake

Rollins Pass

Wilderness Boundary

Wilderness Boundary

N

Miles

0   1   2

of Hessie to the trailhead. The last 0.8 mile of road may not be suitable for low-clearance or two-wheel-drive vehicles.

Key points:
- 0.0   Hessie Trailhead.
- 1.0   Junction with the Devils Thumb and Devils Thumb Bypass Trails. Go right up the Devils Thumb Bypass Trail.
- 1.7   Enter the Indian Peaks Wilderness Boundary.
- 2.1   Junction with the Devils Thumb Trail.
- 3.9   Junction with the Diamond Lake Trail.
- 4.5   Jasper Lake.
- 5.6   Devils Thumb Lake.
- 6.9   Devils Thumb Pass and the Corona Trail.
- 9.4   King Lake Trail.
- 10.1   Bob and Betty Lake Trail.
- 13.9   Devils Thumb Trail.
- 14.9   Back at the Hessie Trailhead.

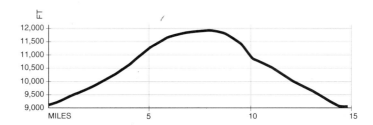

The hike: This is one of my favorite hikes in the state of Colorado. Beautiful trails, excellent campsites, and stunning scenery are the norm on this backcounty excursion. The first part of the hike travels on the Devils Thumb Trail up to the Continental Divide and the Corona Trail. The hike starts from the Hessie Trailhead and travels up an old, rocky roadbed up to the Devils Thumb Bypass Trail. Go right on the Devils Thumb Bypass Trail along the south fork of Middle Boulder Creek to an open meadow and the wilderness boundary. This section of the trail can be extremely wet. (Stay on the main trail and don't cut or make new trails.) With moisture comes wildflowers, and lots of them; take your time and enjoy nature's show.

At the 2.1-mile mark you are back on the Devils Thumb Trail. Here you begin a fairly steep climb up to Jasper Lake on an old road that was once used for mining. You can still see the remnants of the old wooden planks used on this old steep road. This section of the trail stays wet well into summer. The views to the northwest are beautiful and will help to keep your mind off the wet trail and the steep grade.

At the 3.9-mile mark you will pass the Diamond Lake Trail on the right. Continue straight on level tread through some wet meadows dropping down to Jasper Lake. Jasper Lake sits in an impressive position below towering rock walls in a beautiful alpine cirque. The lake is a great place to camp and fish; just remember: Camping is in designated sites along the lake. Continue along the Devils Thumb Trail up into dense spruce forests to Devils Thumb Lake. This is another great spot to camp, fish, or rest a short bit before the steep climb to Devils Thumb Pass and the Corona Trail. This is the last good spot for camping for the next 4 miles, so if you are at all tired and weary, stop here and rest.

The trail up to the pass is steep, narrow, and rocky. Snow remains on the trail well into summer, and the trail tops out at almost 12,000 feet on the top of Devils Thumb Pass. Once you reach the top of the pass, enjoy the panoramic views and the alpine tundra. Drop down to the south and the Corona Trail. The next 2.4 miles of hiking are above timberline and are quite exposed to the elements, so try to be off this trail by early afternoon. Summer thunderstorms can be very violent and dangerous.

The trail is faint in some sections, but be on the lookout for rock cairns sticking up from the alpine tundra leading the way to the King Lake Trail and Rollins Pass. The trail makes a steep drop down to King Lake Trail at the 9.4-mile mark. Go left down the King Lake Trail to King Lake, which is set in a rock cirque just north of Rollins Pass. The lake is stocked with cutthroat and rainbow trout and also offers great camping (by permit only) along the shoreline. From King Lake the trail drops fairly steeply down to the Bob and Betty Lake Trail just after a stream crossing. The trail forks with the left fork leading up to Bob and Betty Lakes. Continue down the King Lake Trail, following the south fork of Middle Boulder Creek to the Devils Thumb Trail in a large open meadow. Here you are just a short 1.1-mile downhill jaunt to the Hessie Trailhead and your car.

Camping: By permit only at Jasper Lake, Devils Thumb Lake, and King Lake. (See Appendix A for permit-issuing locations.)

The top of Devils Thumb Pass.

28 Woodland Lake Trail

Highlights: This is an enjoyable full-day or two-day hike u[..u beautiful Woodland Lake, a small, shallow lake nestled in a valley just north of Woodland Mountain. Wildflowers and alpine scenery are the highlights of this one- to two-day hike. The lake is stocked with cutthroat trout, so bring a fishing rod.

Season: June to late October.

Distance: 4.8 miles one-way.

Difficulty: Moderate.

Map: Trails Illustrated Indian Peaks/Gold Hill, #102.

Management: Boulder Ranger District, USDA Forest Service.

Trail conditions: The lower portion of the trail is maintained and sees heavy use during the late summer months. The rocky upper portion of the hike follows a rock- and tree-filled gulch, crosses a stream, and is extremely wet in the late spring; it remains covered in snow during the late spring and early summer months.

Finding the trailhead: From the junction of SR 93 and SR 119 in Boulder, go west on SR 119 for 16 miles to Nederland. Go south on SR 119 for 0.5 mile to the Eldora turnoff. Go right for 3.2 miles to the town of Eldora. Continue straight for 1.5 miles to a road junction. Go left past the old town site of Hessie to the trailhead. The last 0.8 mile of road may not be suitable for low-clearance or two-wheel-drive vehicles.

Key points:

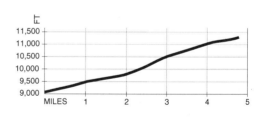

0.0 Hessie Trailhead.

1.0 Junction with the Devils Thumb and Devils Thumb Bypass Trails. Go left over the bridge and follow the Devils Thumb Trail.

1.2 The Lost Lake Trail goes left; Continue straight.

1.4 Cross over a bridge. The King Lake Trail veers to the left. Continue straight.

2.3 Junction with the Woodland Lake Trail. Go left up the narrow, rocky gulch. In late spring and early summer expect to find snow along this section of the trail.

2.9 Cross over the stream on a log bridge. Pass the remnants of a small building and climb steeply up past a waterfall in a dense conifer forest up to level ground. Just before the lake the trail opens into a beautiful stream-fed meadow that is filled with wildflowers and has great views of Woodland Mountain.

4.8 Arrive at Woodland Lake.

The hike: From the trailhead follow the wide four-wheel-drive road up to the Devils Thumb Bypass Trail. This section of the trail climbs gently along

Woodland Lake Trail

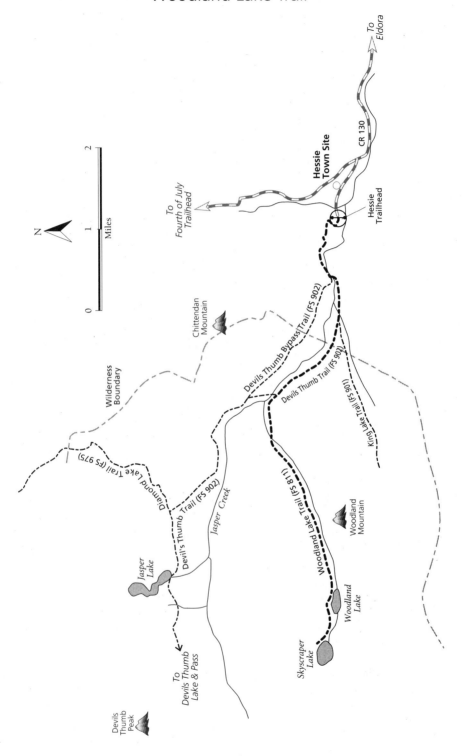

the south fork of Middle Boulder Creek on rocky tread. In the summer the hills along the trail are covered with mountain dryad, nelson larkspur, creeping hollygrape, and yellow stonecrop. After 0.5 mile the trail becomes very rocky and parallels Boulder Creek. There are some rocks on the left that are a great place to stop, relax, and enjoy the rushing waters of Boulder Creek. The runoff waters of late spring and early summer are quite impressive as they flow down from the high peaks.

At the 1.1-mile mark you come to a junction with the Lost Lake Trail. Continue straight up to a bridge and a junction with the King Lake Trail. Follow the Devils Thumb Trail straight in a wide-open meadow into the wilderness area. The trail is smooth and flat and offers panoramic views to the north and west. The trail stays close to Jasper Creek, and in the summer months wildflowers are abundant.

At the 2.3-mile mark you reach the narrow, rocky Woodland Lake Trail. Go left. You will find snow on this part of the trail well into the early summer months. At around the 3-mile mark you cross over the stream on a small log bridge. On the other side of the stream lies the trail and remnants of a small old building. Follow the cairns up past a wet area and small waterfall. This is the most strenuous section of the hike as you gain more than 1,000 feet of elevation in less than 2 miles of hiking.

Just before the lake, at around the 4.5-mile mark, the trail levels out through an open meadow with great views. The lake appears just left of the trail. Take a break and enjoy the lake and the views before you head back to the Hessie Trailhead.

Camping: Camping is allowed by permit only in the Woodland Travel Zone Area. (See Appendix A for permit-issuing locations.)

Entering the Wilderness.

29 King Lake Trail

Highlights:	Alpine lakes, abundant wildflowers, cascading mountain streams, and spectacular views make for a wonderful two-day hike. Don't forget to bring a fishing rod.
Season:	June to late October.
Distance:	5.7 miles one-way.
Difficulty:	Moderate to strenuous.
Map:	Trails Illustrated Indian Peaks/Gold Hill, #102.
Management:	Boulder Ranger District, USDA Forest Service.
Trail conditions:	The lower portion of the trail is maintained and sees heavy use during the late summer months. The middle section of the hike follows along the south fork of Middle Boulder Creek while the upper section makes a steep climb up to the Continental Divide and the Corona Trail.

Finding the trailhead: From the junction of SR 93 and SR 119 in Boulder, go west on SR 119 for 16 miles to Nederland. Go south on SR 119 for 0.5 mile to the Eldora turnoff. Go right for 3.2 miles to the town of Eldora. Continue straight for 1.5 miles to a road junction. Go left past the old town site of Hessie to the trailhead. The last 0.8 mile of road may not be suitable for low-clearance or two-wheel-drive vehicles.

Key points:

0.0   Hessie Trailhead.
1.0   Cross over the south fork of Middle Boulder Creek. Go right past the Lost Lake Trail on the left to the King Lake Trail.
1.3   Junction with the King Lake Trail. Go left.
3.6   Cross over Middle Boulder Creek.
5.0   Junction with the Bob and Betty Lake Trail.
5.4   King Lake on the right.
5.7   Corona Trail and the Continental Divide.

Elevation profile (feet): 11,500 / 11,000 / 10,500 / 10,000 / 9,500 / 9,000 — MILES 1 2 3 4 5 6

The hike: From the Hessie Trailhead follow the obvious wide road up to the south fork of Middle Boulder Creek and the Devils Thumb Bypass Trail. Cross over the creek on a bridge and go right up to the Lost Lake Trail on the left. Continue straight up to an open meadow and the King Lake Trail. There are great views to the west and to Devils Thumb Peak.

Go left on the King Lake Trail and follow along the north side of the creek. Dense spruce forest surrounds the trail, and occasionally you will travel through wet meadows filled with beautiful alpine flowers. The trail climbs at a gradual grade and is quite peaceful with the sounds of the nearby creek.

King Lake Trail

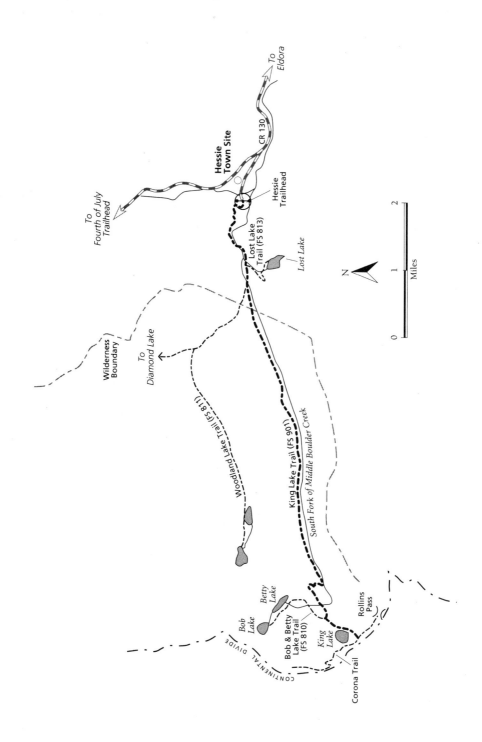

Open meadow at the start of the King Lake Trail.

At the 4.2-mile mark the trail becomes steeper as you climb up to the Bob and Betty Lake Trail. At the 5-mile mark you arrive at a trail junction. The Bob and Betty Lake Trail goes off to the right. Go left, cross over a small stream, and, after some steep hiking, pass King Lake on the right.

Past the lake the trail climbs steeply up to the Continental Divide and the Corona Trail. From a base camp at King Lake you can explore Bob and Betty Lakes, the Corona Trail, and Rollins Pass. Don't forget a fishing rod. The hike up to King Lake is worth every step: It is one of the most beautiful lakes in the Indian Peaks Wilderness Area.

Camping: Camping is allowed by permit only at King Lake, and it is a great place to spend the night.

30 Jenny Creek Trail

Highlights: This is a nice day hike or overnight backpack up to Yankee Doodle Lake via the Jenny Creek Trail, starting at the Eldora Ski Area near the town of Eldora. Wildflowers, mountain streams, and views are the main attractions of this hike along Jenny Creek. This is a great winter ski or snowshoe tour.

Season: May to October.

Distance: 4.9 miles one-way.

Difficulty: Easy to moderate.

Map: Trails Illustrated Indian Peaks/Gold Hill, #102.

Management: Boulder Ranger District, USDA Forest Service.

Trail conditions: The trail is well marked and is narrow in some sections and wide in others.

Finding the trailhead: From the junction of SR 93 and SR 119 in Boulder, go west on SR 119 for 16 miles to Nederland. Go south on SR 119 for 0.5 mile to the Eldora turnoff. Go right for 2.2 miles to a turnoff for the Eldora Ski Area. Turn left, following the signs for Eldora Ski Area. Park in the large parking area near the Nordic Center.

Key points:

1.0	Trail junction.
1.5	Meadow.
2.7	Trail junction.
3.1	Trail junction.
4.7	Trail junction.
4.9	Rollins Pass Road and Yankee Doodle Lake.

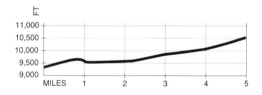

The hike: From the parking area head straight up the service road on the left side of the Ho-Hum ski slope. The trail climbs at a modest incline and has great views northwest to South Arapaho Peak. The trail passes behind a chairlift and heads for the trees and a FOREST ACCESS sign. Power up a short, steep hill, then briefly drop into a small gulch. Climb steeply out of the gulch, arriving at a three-way junction at the top of the hill with a large sign at around the 1-mile mark. Go left, following the sign, then make a quick right back onto the Jenny Creek Trail. The trail drops down toward Jenny Creek into a small open meadow with an old sign marking the trail. This beautiful section of the hike cuts straight through a dense lodgepole forest.

Past the meadow the trail stays fairly level, staying close to the north side of Jenny Creek. The moist area along the creek is host to a number of water-loving flowers, with paintbrush, golden banner, woundwart, and fireweed being the most common. At around the 2.7-mile mark you arrive at a trail junction with the Quinn Mountain Spur Trail branching off to the right. Continue straight past another spur trail that contours around the south side of Quinn Mountain. At the 3.1-mile mark you arrive at another trail junction.

Jenny Creek Trail

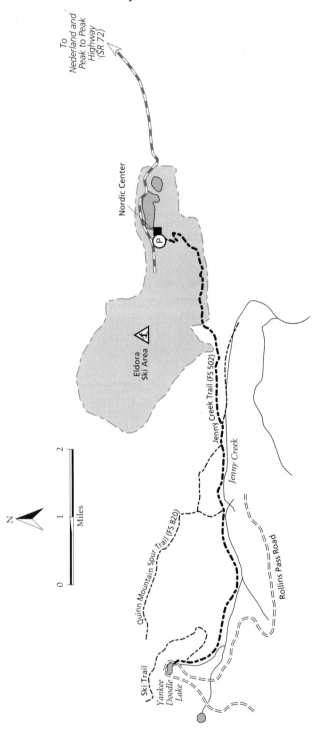

To Nederland and Peak to Peak Highway (SR 72)

Nordic Center

Eldora Ski Area

N

0   1   2
Miles

Jenny Creek Trail (FS 502)

Jenny Creek

Quinn Mountain Spur Trail (FS 820)

Rollins Pass Road

Ski Trail

Yankee Doodle Lake

Bear left on the Jenny Creek Trail and begin a steep climb up to Yankee Doodle Lake and Rollins Pass Road. At around the 4.7-mile mark and just a short distance from Rollins Pass Road there is a trail shooting off to the right. This trail goes north toward Quinn Mountain and eventually winds back to Rollins Pass Road above Yankee Doodle Lake. Feel free to take this trail for added mileage or to connect with the Corona Trail near the top of Rollins Pass. You gain almost 800 feet in the last 1.5 mile of hiking, so save some energy for the return trip.

Camping: Along the trail and near Yankee Doodle Lake.

31 Upper Forest Lakes

Highlights:	This is an easy hike down to alpine lakes and tarns in the Forest Lakes basin, which is located just below Rollins Pass and is a great spot for fishing and picnicking.
Season:	June to late October.
Distance:	0.5 mile to the first lake.
Difficulty:	Easy.
Map:	Trails Illustrated Indian Peaks/Gold Hill, #102.
Management:	Boulder Ranger District, USDA Forest Service.
Trail conditions:	The trail is marked and well-maintained.

Finding the trailhead: From Boulder follow SR 119 through Nederland to Rollinsville. Turn right on CR 16 and travel 7.5 miles along South Boulder Creek to a fork in the road. Go right on CR 149 (Rollins Pass Road) for 11 miles to a parking area just above Jenny Lake at a sharp curve in the road.

Key points:
    0.0   Trailhead.
    0.5   The first Forest Lake.

The hike: Forest Lakes Trail drops down to the first Forest Lake in a mere 0.5 mile. When you arrive at the first lake, a couple of options are available. You can go right around the first lake on a rough trail below towering rock walls and a splashing waterfall. Wildflowers are abundant near the waterfall, and the fishing is quite good in this area of the lake. Another option is to go left at the first lake, to the lower Forest Lakes. This area is filled with wildflowers, lakes, tarns, and bogs. You can easily spend the better part of the day exploring this exceptional alpine basin.

Camping: Along the trail and near the parking area.

Upper Forest Lakes

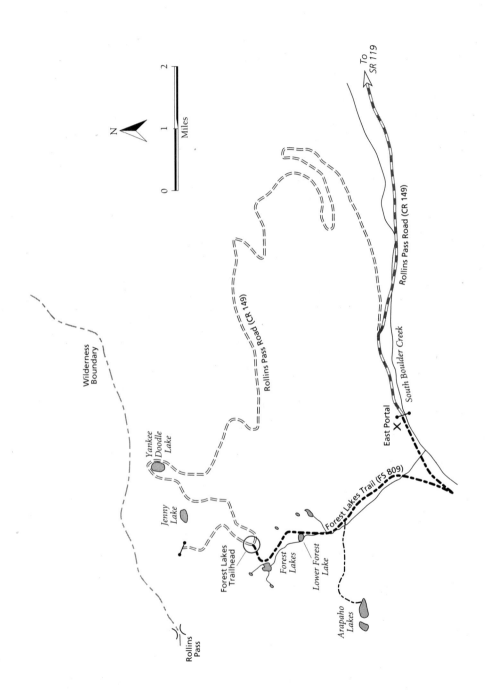

32 Forest Lakes Trail

Highlights: This is a wonderful day hike or two-day backpack trip up to eleven beautiful alpine lakes and tarns located near Rollins Pass and the southern boundary of the Indian Peaks Wilderness Area. Wildflowers, views, and the Forest Lakes are the main attractions of this hike.

Season: June to October.

Distance: 4.2 miles one-way.

Difficulty: Moderate to strenuous.

Map: Trails Illustrated Winter Park/Rollins Pass/Central City, #103.

Management: Boulder Ranger District, USDA Forest Service.

Trail conditions: The lower section of the Forest Lakes Trail (FS 809) is smooth and well maintained. The upper section is rocky, wet, and steep and has several stream crossings.

Finding the trailhead: From Boulder take SR 119 through Nederland to Rollinsville. Turn west (right) on CR 149 and travel 7.5 miles along South Boulder Creek to a fork in the road. Go left for 1 mile to the east portal of the Moffat Tunnel and a large parking area on the left.

Key points:

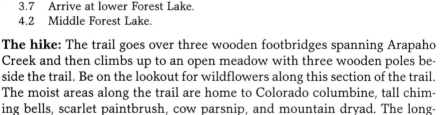

0.0	The trailhead starts just left of Moffat Tunnel.
1.0	Junction with Forest Lakes Trail.
1.6	Cross over Arapaho Creek.
2.2	Cross over Arapaho Creek again.
3.7	Arrive at lower Forest Lake.
4.2	Middle Forest Lake.

The hike: The trail goes over three wooden footbridges spanning Arapaho Creek and then climbs up to an open meadow with three wooden poles beside the trail. Be on the lookout for wildflowers along this section of the trail. The moist areas along the trail are home to Colorado columbine, tall chiming bells, scarlet paintbrush, cow parsnip, and mountain dryad. The long-stem Colorado columbine is the state flower of Colorado and is also one the most beautiful flowers growing in the foothills and mountains of the state.

At the poles go right over a small creek and climb on a wide, smooth trail through a mature spruce forest on a steep slope up to Arapaho Creek. The trail climbs at a modest grade, and the few open areas reveal views to the east, Nebraska Hill, and wildflowers growing on the steep, forested slopes. At the 1.6-mile mark you cross over cascading Arapaho Creek. Depending

Forest Lakes Trail • Heart Lake Trail to James Peak

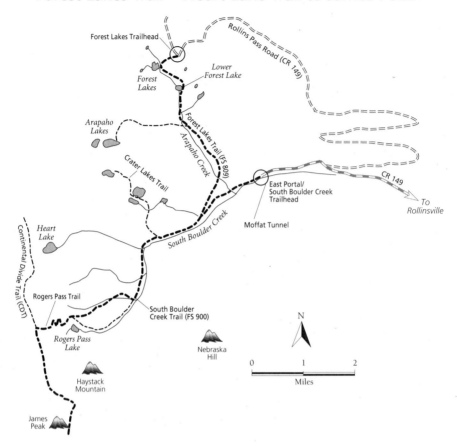

on the time of the year and summer runoff conditions, the creek can be somewhat dangerous to cross. There is a rope strung across the creek to aid in fording, but I recommend crossing the creek on a log bridge 50 feet below the trail.

Past the creek the trail climbs steeply up to a meadow. The main trail goes through a wet, marshy area up to Arapaho Creek. You can avoid the wet area by taking a spur trail on the right that winds above the marsh and meets the main trail before crossing Arapaho Creek. Wildflowers are abundant around the marsh, and the colors are quite spectacular in midsummer.

At the 2.2-mile mark you ford Arapaho Creek again and follow a faint trail that stays close to the creek. The trail becomes quite steep and is somewhat hard to follow. There are several downed trees on the trail. Remember to stay close to the main drainage and be on the lookout for rock cairns to guide you.

At around the 3-mile mark the trail gains a shelf in a large open meadow. The trail slices through a stand of krummholz pines and into a meadow with beautiful open views of the surrounding rocky peaks. The terrain below the

Wildflowers near Forest Lakes.

peaks is quite steep and retains snow—the source of water for the surrounding lakes and streams—most of the year. The trail climbs above the open meadow and passes a large boulder field on the right into alpine tundra. The soft grasses of the tundra make a great place to set up camp if you are backpacking. From here it is just a short jaunt up to lower Forest Lake. There is a rough trail that skirts the north side of lower Forest Lake and leads up to upper Forest Lake, where the trail climbs steeply up to the Forest Lakes Trailhead that is located on Rollins Pass Road.

Camping: Along the trail and at lower Forest Lake.

Heart Lake Trail to James Peak

See Map on Page 98

Highlights: This is a wonderful two-day hike up to James Peak (13,294 feet) and two beautiful alpine lakes just outside the southern boundary of the Indian Peaks Wilderness Area. Heart and Rogers Pass Lakes are situated in an alpine valley below the jagged, rocky summits of Haystack Mountain and James Peak.

Season: Late June to October.

Distance: 7.2 miles one-way.

Difficulty: Moderate.

Map: Trails Illustrated Winter Park/Rollins Pass/Central City, #103.

Management: Boulder Ranger District, USDA Forest Service.

Trail conditions: The lower section of the Heart Lake Trail has smooth tread and is wet in some spots. The upper section of the trail is wet, very rocky, and filled with roots and downed trees.

Finding the trailhead: From Boulder take SR 119 through Nederland to Rollinsville. Turn west (right) on CR 149 and travel 7.5 miles along South Boulder Creek to a fork in the road. Go left for 1 mile to the east portal of the Moffat Tunnel and a large parking area on the left.

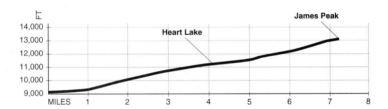

Key points:

0.0	The trailhead starts just left of Moffat Tunnel.
0.4	Arapaho Creek goes off to the right.
0.8	A trail goes right to Forest Lakes.
2.1	Cross over South Boulder Creek.
4.2	Arrive at Heart Lake. Go left on the Rogers Pass Trail.
5.2	On top of Rogers Pass.
7.2	Summit of James Peak.

The hike: Heart and Rogers Pass Lakes are situated in an alpine valley below the jagged, rocky summits of Haystack Mountain and James Peak. The trail up to the lakes takes a direct line up a rocky and wet gulch along South Boulder Creek. From the parking area go left over South Boulder Creek just before the Moffat Tunnel to the trailhead and a kiosk. Follow the well-marked trail past the kiosk up along South Boulder Creek. The trail crosses three wooden footbridges over Arapaho Creek up a to meadow with a pair of abandoned cabins. At the meadow there are three wooden posts on the trail. To the right is the Forest Lakes Trail; continue straight and begin a steep climb on rocky, rooted, wet tread up a rock-infested gully. The trail follows a line along the north side of South Boulder Creek in a dense, mature spruce forest. The spruce trees are draped with moss, and the trail follows an old abandoned mining road.

At the 2.1-mile mark the trail becomes level and angles left through an extremely wet section littered with beautiful wildflowers. The trail is somewhat hard to follow in this section and crosses an occasional wooden plank in the wetter sections. Just remember that you want to follow South Boulder Creek and look for the red dot on the trees.

The trail becomes rocky and steep as you gain altitude on your way up to Heart Lake. You are deep in a dense spruce forest along this section of the trail, but there is the occasional open area that reveals views out to Nebraska Hill and a ridgeline leading up to Haystack Mountain. I hiked this trail in early June, and the upper section still had a fair amount of snow, which made route-finding somewhat difficult.

Upon arrival at the lake, set up camp and take a well-deserved rest. If you are planning to climb James Peak, set up camp at the lake, spend the night, and climb James Peak early in the morning. From the lake follow the obvious Rogers Pass Trail, which climbs steeply up to the Continental Divide Trail (CDT). Gain the Continental Divide Trail and drop to the left along Haystack Mountain. Climb up to a saddle, remaining on the Continental Divide Trail. At the saddle the Continental Divide Trail continues straight to Berthoud Pass and beyond. Follow the obvious rock cairns up the steep talus slope to the summit. The slope is exposed to thunderstorms, so make sure

East portal of the Moffat Tunnel.

you are off the summit by noon. The views from the top of James Peak are well worth the effort and extend in all directions. After a rest, retrace your route back to Heart Lake.

Camping: At Heart Lake.

34 Roaring Fork Trail

Highlights:	This is a great backcountry trip into the Roaring Fork drainage and Hell Canyon. Throw in a couple of beautiful alpine lakes, wildflowers, and spectacular views, and you have one of the best trips in the western Indian Peaks.
Season:	June to October.
Distance:	6.8 miles one-way.
Difficulty:	Moderate to strenuous.
Map:	Trails Illustrated Indian Peaks/Gold Hill, #102.
Management:	Sulphur Ranger District, USDA Forest Service.
Trail conditions:	Rocky and steep in some sections.

Finding the trailhead: From Granby follow SR 34 north to the entrance of the Arapaho National Recreation Area. Go east on FR 125 for 10 miles to the Arapaho Bay Campground. Turn left and go 0.5 mile to the Roaring Fork Trailhead on the right.

Key points:
- 0.5 Steep switchbacks.
- 1.0 Cross over Roaring Fork Creek.
- 2.4 Trail junction.
- 4.0 Views.
- 4.5 Saddle.
- 6.3 Stone Lake.
- 6.8 Upper Lake.

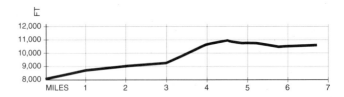

The hike: From the trailhead follow the Roaring Fork Trail east to where it splits with the Knight Ridge Trail. Go right on the Roaring Fork Trail into the Indian Peaks Wilderness Area and begin a steep climb up a series of long switchbacks. The trail stays steep for 0.5 mile of strenuous hiking, gaining 700 feet of elevation up to a log bridge over Roaring Fork Creek. Your legs should be tired after that steep start.

Roaring Fork Trail

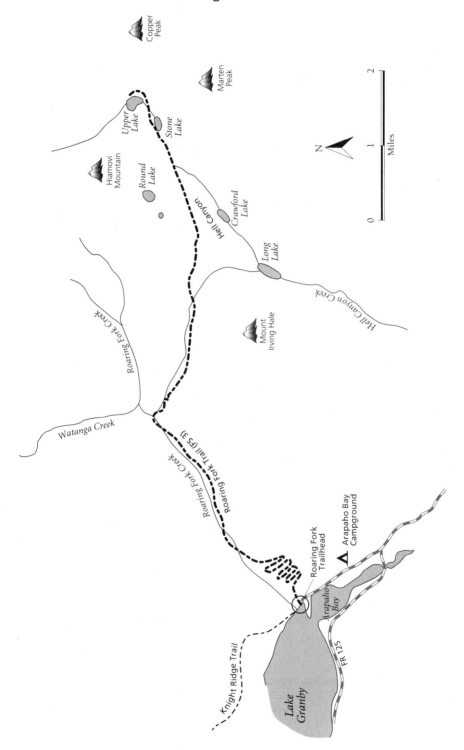

Angle right over the bridge and follow the trail along Roaring Fork Creek at a much more pleasant grade to Watanga Creek. The trail goes southeast past Watanga Creek and begins a very long, steep climb up to a saddle with stunning views west to the rocky summit of Mount Irving Hale (11,754 feet) and Hell Canyon to the south. This is a good spot to regroup and take a well-deserved rest.

From this point the trail makes a dramatic drop down into Hell Canyon via steep, narrow switchbacks to level ground surrounded by beautiful flower-filled alpine meadows. There are a number of downed trees on the descent, and you lose almost 600 feet of elevation in less than a mile of hiking. The trail now travels through wet meadows deep in spectacular Hell Canyon to Stone Lake. The trail remains level but becomes hard to follow in the wet areas.

At Stone Lake the trail all but disappears on the way to Upper Lake. Try to pick the best line through the boulders. From here it is just a short hop, skip, and jump to Upper Lake. Hiamovi Mountain (12,395 feet) and Hiamovi Tower (12,220 feet), spectacular rocky summits, dominate the skyline to the north. The almost twin mountains are a mere 0.25 mile from the southern boundary of Rocky Mountain National Park and sit in an impressive position above the lakes. The southeast buttress of Hiamovi Tower is particularly impressive and rises nearly 1,400 rocky feet from Stone Lake to its pointed, alpine summit. The camping here is as good as it gets in the Indian Peaks, and there is also good trout fishing at both lakes.

Camping: At Arapaho Bay Campground, along the trail, and at Stone and Upper Lakes.

---

35 Cascade Creek Trail to Crater Lake

Highlights:	This is an exciting backpacking trip into one of the most beautiful alpine cirques in the Indian Peaks Wilderness Area. Waterfalls, wildflowers, spruce and lodgepole pine forests, and beautiful Crater Lake are the main attractions of this backcountry trip. Bring a fishing rod and try your luck at Monarch, Mirror, or Crater Lakes.
Season:	June to October.
Distance:	7.6 miles one-way.
Difficulty:	Moderate to strenuous.
Map:	Trails Illustrated Indian Peaks/Gold Hill, #102.
Management:	Sulphur Ranger District, USDA Forest Service.
Trail conditions:	The lower portion of the trail is well traveled, the trail to Crater Lake is rocky and wet in several sections, and the upper sections of the trail hold snow well into June.

Cascade Creek Trail to Crater Lake

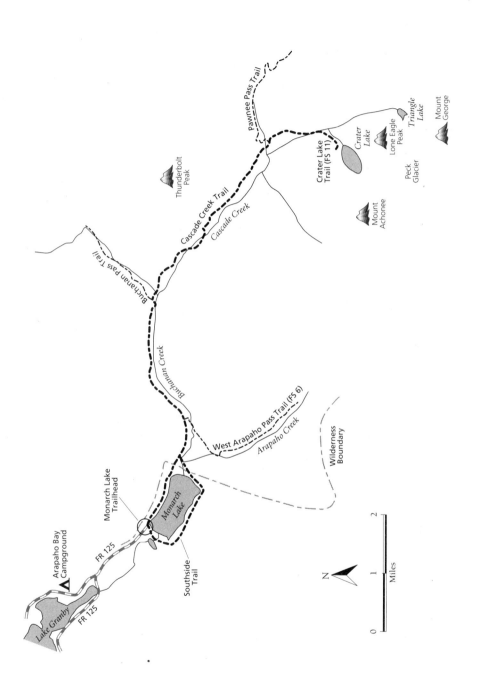

Finding the trailhead: From Granby follow SR 34 north to the entrance of the Arapaho National Recreation Area. Go east on FR 125 for 10.2 miles to the Monarch Lake Trailhead.

Key points:
1.5   Southside Trail.
3.4   Buchanan Pass Trail.
4.9   Cascade Falls.
6.3   Junction of the Pawnee Pass Trail and the Crater Lake Trail.
7.6   Crater Lake.

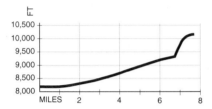

The hike: Beautiful backcountry excursions don't get much better than this. The hike starts at the Monarch Lake Trailhead at the north end of Monarch Lake. The trail is fairly level as you travel into the wilderness boundary and up to a trail junction with great views of the lake on the right. After 1.5 miles of easy hiking you arrive at a junction with the Southside Trail, which goes right and hugs the shoreline of Monarch Lake back to the trailhead. This makes for a beautiful short hike around Monarch Lake.

Continue on the Cascade Creek Trail and cross a bridge over a stream draining from the rugged Hell Canyon on the left. The trail climbs up several switchbacks, gaining level ground through a beautiful lodgepole forest above Buchanan Creek on the right. At the junction with the Buchanan Pass Trail, go right on the Cascade Creek Trail, cross Cascade Creek, and then hike up to Cascade Falls, a gorgeous waterfall nestled below the impressive Thunderbolt Peak (11,938 feet). Past the falls the trail travels through several wet meadows filled with an array of wildflowers and spectacular views to the east. The trail is now on the north side of Cascade Creek and stays fairly moderate up to a junction with the Pawnee Pass and Crater Lake Trails.

Go right on the Crater Lake Trail into a dense spruce forest along the east side of Cascade Creek. In a short distance you arrive at an unmarked trail junction. Go left and up to a stream with a log footbridge. Cross over the bridge and climb up to Mirror Lake on the left. Continue for a short distance up to Crater Lake and your destination. The trail terminates near the midpoint of the lake, and Lone Eagle Peak towers above the lake. The mountain was named after Charles Lindbergh, the first person to fly an airplane across the Atlantic Ocean.

Camping: By permit only at designated campsites along the trail and at Mirror and Crater Lakes.

36 West Arapaho Pass Trail to Caribou Lake

Highlights: Waterfalls, wildflowers, spruce and lodgepole pine forests, and beautiful Caribou Lake are the main attractions of this wonderful backcountry trip. Bring a fishing rod and try your luck at Monarch or Caribou Lakes.

Season: June to October.

Distance: 9.1 miles one-way.

Difficulty: Moderate to strenuous.

Map: Trails Illustrated Indian Peaks/Gold Hill, #102.

Management: Sulphur Ranger District, USDA Forest Service.

Trail conditions: The trail varies from smooth, level tread to extremely rocky and steep.

Finding the trailhead: From Granby follow SR 34 north to the entrance of the Arapaho National Recreation Area. Go east on FR 125 for 10.2 miles to the Monarch Lake Trailhead.

Key points:
- 1.5 Southside Trail.
- 2.0 West Arapaho Pass Trail.
- 4.5 Stream crossing.
- 6.0 Stream crossing.
- 7.5 Stream crossing.
- 8.2 Coyote Park.
- 9.1 Caribou Lake.

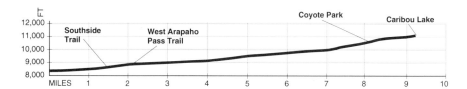

The hike: The hike starts at the Monarch Lake Trailhead at the north end of Monarch Lake. The trail is fairly level as you travel into the wilderness boundary and up to a trail junction with great views of the lake on the right. After 1.5 miles of easy hiking you arrive at a junction with the Southside Trail, which goes right and hugs the shoreline of Monarch Lake back to the trailhead. This is a beautiful hike around Monarch Lake if you are looking for a short day hike.

Go right on the Southside Trail for 0.5 mile, traveling over a large footbridge over Arapaho Creek to a junction with the West Arapaho Pass Trail. Go left on the West Arapaho Pass Trail and climb up several switchbacks above the eastside of the creek. This section of the trail travels through a dense, beautiful spruce forest and gains about 500 feet of elevation in the first mile.

West Arapaho Pass Trail to Caribou Lake

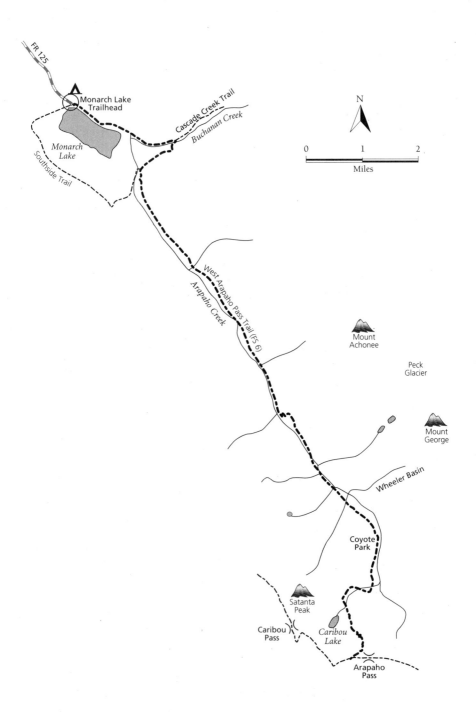

FR 125

Monarch Lake
Trailhead

Cascade Creek Trail

Buchanan Creek

Monarch
Lake

Southside Trail

West Arapaho Pass Trail (FS 6)

Arapaho Creek

N

0   1   2
Miles

Mount
Achonee

Peck
Glacier

Mount
George

Wheeler Basin

Coyote
Park

Satanta
Peak

Caribou
Pass

Caribou
Lake

Arapaho
Pass

The next 4 miles of hiking are quite pleasant as the trail drops down Arapaho Creek then climbs away from it. You will cross over several small creeks that drain from an alpine lake to the east. After crossing a log bridge over Arapaho Creek, the trail climbs up to Coyote Park, an open, beautiful meadow with spectacular views to the east, north, and south. South and North Arapaho Peaks tower to the east, and Mount George and Apache Peak fill the skyline to the north. This is an excellent spot to camp if you are feeling a little tired.

The next mile of hiking climbs up to a shelf, gaining 800 feet in elevation, and Caribou Lake. Caribou Lake sits in an impressive valley below lofty mountain peaks and Caribou and Arapaho Passes. This is one of the prettiest spots in the entire Indian Peaks, so plan on staying a few days. Bring your fishing rod and camera.

Options: From a base camp at Caribou Lake, you can climb up Arapaho Pass to Lake Dorothy or follow the Arapaho Pass Trail down to the Arapaho Glacier Trail and climb North and South Arapaho Peaks.

Camping: By permit only along the trail and at Caribou Lake.

37 Columbine Lake Trail

Highlights:	You'll see wildflowers, an alpine lake, and stunning views on this great day hike, which is suitable for the whole family.
Season:	May to late October.
Distance:	4.3 miles one-way.
Difficulty:	Easy to moderate.
Map:	Trails Illustrated Indian Peaks/Gold Hill, #102.
Management:	Sulphur Ranger District, USDA Forest Service.
Trail conditions:	The lower section of the trail up to the Columbine Lake Trail is very popular and maintained. The Columbine Lake Trail is initially smooth and becomes quite rocky near the lake.

Finding the trailhead: From Winter Park follow US 40 north to CR 83. Go right on CR 83 for 0.8 mile. Turn left on CR 84 and follow it to FR 129. Go north on FR 129 for 11 miles following the signs for Indian Peaks Wilderness access and Meadow Creek Reservoir. Park at the Junco Trailhead parking area.

Key points:
- 1.3 Abandoned cabin on the right.
- 1.5 Indian Peaks Wilderness boundary.

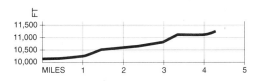

Columbine Lake Trail • Caribou Pass Trail

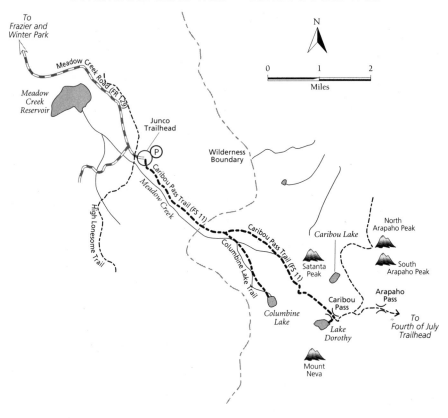

1.9 Junction with the Columbine Lake Trail.
2.9 Trail becomes steep and rocky.
4.3 Columbine Lake.

The hike: This family-friendly hike travels up to a beautiful alpine lake nestled in a valley below towering rock walls. The hike starts at the Junco Trailhead and follows the Caribou Pass Trail up to the Columbine Lake Trail. The first part of the trail follows a wide path through a forest of beautiful spruce trees and lodgepole pines. Cross over a small wooden bridge and go about 0.6 mile to another small stream crossing. After the second stream crossing the trail becomes extremely rocky and steep. Look for alpine daisy, paintbrush, and black-eyed Susan, which grow profusely along the trail.

At the 1.3-mile mark you come to an old abandoned cabin on the right, about 50 feet from the trail. Past the cabin the trail levels off, and at the 1.5-mile mark is a sign marking the Indian Peaks Wilderness boundary. To the right of the sign, Meadow Creek flows down through a meadow filled with willows, marsh grasses, and wildflowers. Views open up to the south and

Flower-filled meadow on the Columbine Lake Trail.

east, with Mount Neva and Caribou Pass looming straight ahead. Continue straight for 0.3 mile to a junction with the Columbine Lake Trail, which goes right into a large, open meadow. This is a great place to set up camp and explore the trails in the area if you will be hiking more than one day.

The trail stays level in the meadow, and views open up to Caribou Pass and Mount Neva. After a short stretch the trail enters a dense spruce forest with Meadow Creek on the right. The trail becomes steeper in the forest and then levels off in a meadow. Near a stream the trail climbs again up through a rocky area. Near the end of the rocky area the grade eases and travels through a meadow up to the lake.

Camping: Along the trail, near the parking area, and by Columbine Lake (by permit only; campfires prohibited).

38 Caribou Pass Trail

See Map on Page 110

Highlights: Wildflowers, alpine lakes, and airy views from Caribou Pass are the main attractions of this hike. The last section of the hike to Lake Dorothy is a steep, narrow ledge cut across the northern flank of Mount Neva.

Season: Late June to October.

Distance: 4.3 miles one-way.

Difficulty: Strenuous.

Map: Trails Illustrated Indian Peaks/Gold Hill, #102.

Management: Sulphur Springs Ranger District, USDA Forest Service.

Trail conditions: The lower section of the trail up to the Columbine Trail is maintained, and the upper portion is steep and narrow, with steep drop-offs. Hikers with vertigo should avoid this last part of the hike.

Finding the trailhead: From Winter Park follow US 40 north to CR 83. Go right on CR 83 for 0.8 mile. Turn left on CR 84 and follow it to FR 129. Go north on FR 129 for 11 miles following the signs for Indian Peaks Wilderness access and Meadow Creek Reservoir. Park at the Junco Trailhead parking area.

Key points:

1.3 Abandoned cabin on the right.

1.5 Indian Peaks Wilderness boundary.

1.9 Junction with the Columbine Lake Trail.

3.4 Caribou Pass.

4.3 Lake Dorothy.

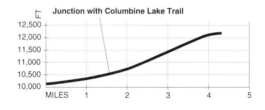

The hike: This is a wonderful hike up to one of the more dramatic passes in the Indian Peaks Wilderness Area. At the end of the climb you are rewarded with beautiful scenery and Lake Dorothy, a stunning alpine lake. Situated at 12,061 feet, it is the highest lake in the Indian Peaks. The trail starts at the Junco Trailhead, and the first portion follows a wide path through a forest of beautiful spruce and lodgepole pine. Cross over a small wooden bridge and travel about 0.6 mile to another small stream crossing, after which the trail becomes extremely rocky and steep. Be on the lookout for alpine daisy, paintbrush, and black-eyed Susan.

At the 1.3-mile mark you come to an old abandoned cabin on the right, 50 feet from the trail. Past the cabin the trail levels off, and at the 1.5-mile mark is a sign marking the Indian Peaks Wilderness boundary. To the right of the sign, Meadow Creek flows down from Columbine Lake through a large, open meadow. Views open up to the south and east, with Mount Neva and Caribou Pass looming straight ahead. Continue straight for 0.3 mile to

Looking west across Caribou Pass.

a junction with the Columbine Lake Trail, which goes right into another large meadow. This is a great place to set up camp and explore the trails in the area if you will be hiking more than one day.

At the trail junction the Caribou Pass Trail goes left up a steep hillside to an open meadow filled with alpine daisy, mountain parsley, paintbrush, and rose gentian, which light up the meadow with their brilliant colors. Satanta Peak (11,979 feet) is northeast of the meadow. The trail remains level for a short distance then climbs steeply up to another meadow. The views to the south, east, and west are breathtaking. Looking back to the west you can see Meadow Creek Reservoir and the Gore Mountain range in the western horizon.

The climbing begins in earnest above the meadow, and the trail becomes quite steep as you power your way up into open tundra below the pass. Keep those legs moving and in no time you'll arrive at Caribou Pass (11,851 feet). Take a break and enjoy the panoramic views in all directions. At this point you can easily go north (left) for 0.6 mile to reach the summit of Satanta Peak, from which there are gorgeous views down to Caribou Lake and Coyote Park. Looking farther north, Mount George (12,876 feet), Apache Peak (13,441 feet), and Arikaree Peak (13,150 feet) fill the skyline with their jagged, rocky summits.

At the pass go south for a short distance and follow the trail below the northern flank of Mount Neva. Here the trail becomes quite narrow and traverses over to Lake Dorothy and Arapaho Pass. Note that this section of the trail has steep drop-offs, is very narrow, and can be a problem for people not accustomed to heights. Use caution and gingerly make you way over toward Arapaho Pass. At the post go right to Lake Dorothy and take a break along the shore of this beautiful alpine lake. Looking east, North Arapaho Peak (13,502 feet) and South Arapaho Peak (13,397 feet) rest impressively above Arapaho Pass and the Glacier Rim Trail. The lake, which is home to cutthroat trout (bring your fishing rod), sits in a majestic position below the towering summit of Mount Neva, whose steep, rocky cliffs surround the lake to the north, west, and south. Take a break and enjoy this beautiful alpine environment before undertaking the long downhill back to the trailhead.

Camping: Along the trail and near the parking area.

Appendix A: Resources

American Hiking Society
1422 Fenwick Lane
Silver Spring, MD 20910
(301) 565-6704

Boulder Area Trails Coalition (BATCO)
Boulder, CO
(303) 441-5262
http://bcn.boulder.co.us/batco

Boulder Convention and Visitors
 Center
2440 Pearl Street
Boulder, CO 80302
(800) 444-0447
www.bouldercoloradousa.com

Boulder Ranger District
USDA Forest Service
2140 Yarmouth Avenue
Boulder, CO 80301
(303) 541-2500

Colorado Division of Wildlife
6060 Broadway
Denver, CO 80216
(303) 297-1192

Colorado Mountain Club
2530 West Alameda Avenue
Denver, CO 80219
(303) 922-8315

Continental Divide Trail Alliance
P.O. Box 628
Pine, CO 80470
(303) 838-3760
www.CDTrail.org

Department of Interior
1849 C Street NW
Washington, DC 20240
www.doi.gov

Estes Park Office
(permit-issuing location)
USDA Forest Service
161 Second Street
Estes Park, CO 80517

Fish and Wildlife Service
Regional Office
134 Union Boulevard
Lakewood, CO 80288
(303) 236-7904
www.r6.fws.gov

Indian Peaks Ace Hardware
(permit-issuing location)
20 Lakeview Drive
Nederland, CO 80466
(303) 258-3132

Mountain Sports
821 Pearl Street
Boulder, CO 80302
(303) 442-8355
www.mospo.com

Nederland Chamber of Commerce
RTD Parking Lot
Nederland, CO 80446
(303) 258-3936
www.nederlandchamber.org

Neptune Mountaineering
633 South Broadway, Unit A
Boulder, CO 80302
(303) 499-8866
www.neptunemountaineering.com

Sulphur Ranger District
USDA Forest Service
9 Ten Mile Drive
P.O. Box 10
Granby, CO 80446
(970) 887-4100

Trails Illustrated Maps
P.O. Box 4357
Evergreen, CO 80439-3746
(303) 670-3457 or (800) 962-1643

Western States Geological Survey
USGS
Western Distribution Branch
P.O. Box 25286
Denver Federal Center
Denver, CO 80225

Appendix B: The Hiker's Checklist

If you've ever hiked into the backcountry and discovered that you've forgotten something essential, you know that it's a good idea to make a checklist and check the items off as you pack. Here are some ideas:

Clothing
- ☐ Dependable rain parka
- ☐ Rain pants
- ☐ Windbreaker
- ☐ Thermal underwear
- ☐ Shorts
- ☐ Long pants or sweatpants
- ☐ Wool cap or balaclava
- ☐ Hat
- ☐ Wool shirt or sweater
- ☐ Jacket or parka
- ☐ Extra socks
- ☐ Underwear
- ☐ Lightweight shirts
- ☐ T-shirts
- ☐ Bandanna(s)
- ☐ Mittens or gloves
- ☐ Belt

Footwear
- ☐ Sturdy, comfortable boots
- ☐ Lightweight camp shoes

Bedding
- ☐ Sleeping bag
- ☐ Foam pad or air mattress
- ☐ Ground sheet (plastic or nylon)
- ☐ Dependable tent

Cooking
- ☐ 1-quart container (plastic)
- ☐ 1-gallon water container for camp use (collapsible)
- ☐ Backpack stove and extra fuel
- ☐ Funnel
- ☐ Aluminum foil
- ☐ Cooking pots
- ☐ Bowls/plates
- ☐ Utensils (spoons, forks, small spatula, knife)
- ☐ Pot scrubber
- ☐ Matches in waterproof container

Food and Drink
- ☐ Cereal
- ☐ Bread
- ☐ Crackers
- ☐ Cheese
- ☐ Trail mix
- ☐ Margarine
- ☐ Powdered soups
- ☐ Salt/pepper
- ☐ Main-course meals
- ☐ Snacks
- ☐ Hot chocolate
- ☐ Tea
- ☐ Powdered milk
- ☐ Drink mixes

Photography
- ☐ Camera and film
- ☐ Filters
- ☐ Lens brush/paper

Miscellaneous
- ☐ Backpack and/or day pack
- ☐ Sunglasses
- ☐ Map and compass
- ☐ Toilet paper
- ☐ Pocketknife
- ☐ Sunscreen
- ☐ Good insect repellent
- ☐ Lip balm
- ☐ Flashlight with good batteries and a spare bulb
- ☐ Candle(s)
- ☐ First-aid kit
- ☐ Small garden trowel or shovel
- ☐ Water filter or purification tablets
- ☐ Plastic bags (for trash)
- ☐ Soap
- ☐ Towel
- ☐ Toothbrush
- ☐ Fishing license
- ☐ Fishing rod, reel, lures, flies, etc.
- ☐ Binoculars
- ☐ Waterproof covering for pack
- ☐ Watch
- ☐ Sewing kit

About the Author

Bob D'Antonio lives in Louisville, Colorado, with his wife, Laurel, and his three children. He is a native of Philadelphia, Pennsylvania, and has spent many hours hiking, climbing, and biking throughout the United States.

Bob's previous FalconGuides include: *Rock Climbing Colorado's San Luis Valley; Classic Rock Climbs #04 Garden of the Gods/Pikes Peak, Colorado; Classic Rock Climbs #03 Mueller State Park/Elevenmile Canyon, Colorado; Mountain Biking Denver/Boulder; Mountain Biking Aspen; Mountain Biking Grand Junction and Fruita;* and *Mountain Biking Greater Philadelphia.*

WHAT'S SO SPECIAL ABOUT UNSPOILED, NATURAL PLACES?

Beauty   Solitude   Wildness   Freedom   Quiet   Adventure
Serenity   Inspiration   Wonder   Excitement
Relaxation   Challenge

There's a lot to love about our treasured public lands, and the reasons are different for each of us. Whatever your reasons are, the national **Leave No Trace** education program will help you discover special outdoor places, enjoy them, and preserve them—today and for those who follow. By practicing and passing along these simple principles, you can help protect the special places you love from being loved to death.

THE PRINCIPLES OF **LEAVE NO TRACE**

- Plan ahead and prepare
- Travel and camp on durable surfaces
- Dispose of waste properly
- Leave what you find
- Minimize campfire impacts
- Respect wildlife
- Be considerate of other visitors

Leave No Trace is a national nonprofit organization dedicated to teaching responsible outdoor recreation skills and ethics to everyone who enjoys spending time outdoors.

To learn more or to become a member, please visit us at www.LNT.org or call (800) 332–4100.

Leave No Trace, P.O. Box 997, Boulder, CO 80306